RODGER WARD

SUPERSTAR OF AMERICAN RACING'S GOLDEN AGE

MIKE O'LEARY

MOTORBOOKS

First published in 2006 by Motorbooks, an imprint of MBI Publishing Company, Galtier Plaza, Suite 200, 380 Jackson Street, St. Paul, MN 55101-3885 USA

The information in this book is true and complete to the best of our knowledge. All recommendations are made without any guarantee on the part of the author or Publisher, who also disclaim any liability incurred in connection with the use of this data or specific details.

We recognize, further, that some words, model names, and designations mentioned herein are the property of the trademark holder. We use them for identification purposes only. This is not an official publication.

MBI Publishing Company titles are also available at discounts in bulk quantity for industrial or sales-promotional use. For details write to Special Sales Manager at MBI Publishing Company, Galtier Plaza, Suite 200, 380 Jackson Street, St. Paul, MN 55101-3885 USA

Library of Congress Cataloging-in-Publication Data

O'Leary, Mike, 1950 Feb. 10-
     Rodger Ward : superstar of American racing's golden age / Mike O'Leary.
        p. cm.
     Includes bibliographical references and index.
     ISBN-13: 978-0-7603-2177-5 (hardbound)
     ISBN-10: 0-7603-2177-9 (hardbound)
  1. Ward, Rodger. 2. Automobile racing drivers--United States--Biography. I. Title.
     GV1032.W38.O553 2006
     796.72092--dc22

                                        2006016254

On the cover, main: One of the traditions of the Indianapolis 500 is the official photo session for the winner on the morning after the race. *Armin Krueger*

Inset: Rodger with Bob Wilke (left) and A. J. Watson (right) in the pits at Indy, 1960. *Armin Krueger*

On the endpapers: Line Drawings by Steve Manning

On the frontispiece: Rodger at the 1964 Hoosier Hundred. No one realized it at the time, but he would only run one more championship race on dirt. *Ken Coles*

On the title pages: Rodger in M. A. Walker's new Kutis at Indy in 1953. *Author collection*

On the back cover: Indianapolis, 1962. Victory lane is a busy place. Especially when it's your second visit. *Rodger Ward Jr.*

Editor: James Michels
Designer: Christopher Fayers

Printed in China

Contents

Foreword

By Chris Economaki, Editor and Publisher Emeritus, *National Speed Sport News*

To which form of auto racing does Rodger Ward rightfully belong? The book you are about to read will help you make that determination. Was it Indy cars? Was it midgets? Was it stock cars? What, exactly, was it? Mike O'Leary's exhaustively researched handiwork will help you decide.

Rodger Ward first came into prominence as a winner in the Indianapolis 500, capturing America's greatest auto race on two occasions. Along the way he secured a national championship in stock car racing—certainly not his specialty—and mastered the art of midget racing. Despite his Indy and stock car triumphs, Ward's highest accolades came at the wheel of midget racing cars, in every case rare and extraordinary.

His first national recognition was shared with his mount, a Ford V8-60-engined midget racing car owned by Vic Edelbrock. It was at the wheel of this underpowered machine that he became the first—and only—non-Offenhauser-engined driver to capture a feature event at Gilmore Stadium, a Los Angeles-based speed palace constructed expressly for the small-car sport. His triumph was described as "unbelievable," however credit was shared with his machine.

A few years later when the first U.S. Grand Prix was contested on Sebring's road course, close examination of the entry regulations revealed a midget racing car could take on the Formula 1 giants of Europe, and Ward was there to do just that. Though his brave and bold try in an oval track car with no transmission was abortive, he earned credit and respect for his challenge.

But another drive, in yet another midget, brought him more fame and wider recognition than either of his Indy 500 triumphs. Ward's victory in a Formula Libre (run what you brung) race at Connecticut's Lime Rock Park road circuit in a run-of-the mill oval track Offenhauser (Offy) midget against Italian Grand Prix cars and big-bore British sports-racing machines brought him not fortune but fame that is looked upon today as the greatest achievement by a midget-racing driver in the sport's history.

But there's more, so read on. . . .

Acknowledgments

This book is the product of more than a year and a half of devoted effort and the assistance of quite a few special people. I would like to offer my gratitude to those who unselfishly shared their time, interviews, photos, details, stories, and suggestions. All are champions to me. At the top of the list is Rodger Ward's family, and in particular Rodger Ward Jr. who sat through hours of interviews, phone calls, and unending questions.

Also topping my list is my wife, Sandi, for her understanding and patience, as well as her painstaking organization and documentation of the photos. And as he has for more than five decades, my father, Ray O'Leary, provided a steadying hand and precise editorial guidance.

Other champions whose contributions were invaluable include: A. J. Watson; Dick Wallen; Don Radbruch; Len Sutton; Andy Casale; Gordon White; Donald Davidson; Jim Haines and the Indianapolis Motor Speedway Photo Shop; Jim Chini; William LaDow; Suzanne Wise and the Stock Car Racing Collection of the Belk Library at Appalachian State University; Rex Dean; Ed Watson; Buzz Rose; Fred Chaparro; Steve Zautke; Gene Crucean; Roy C. Morris; Rosie Rousell; Bob Lawrence; Tom Saal; Terry Reed; Ken Coles; The Greenfield Gallery's Ralph Hibbard Jr. for dipping into the Armin Krueger collection; and Marty Little. Certainly not to be left out are Peter Bodensteiner, who originally sold the idea, and Jim Michels, the highly capable and understanding editor at MBI Publishing Company who kept all of the plates spinning.

Introduction

On the surface, this book attempts to document Rodger Ward's life and racing career. But below that surface lies the story of an era of American auto racing that can never be re-created. While the necessary elements of Rodger's birth, his family, and his days as a youth are touched on lightly, the story that is the focus of this effort begins with the conclusion of World War II.

Rodger Ward's accomplishments as a racer were the product of years of hard work, low pay, mediocre cars, heartbreak, disappointments, bad decisions, picking lettuce, and selling used cars. Included in the same equation were his persistence, willingness to pay his dues, road trips with miracle-working mechanics, and his ability to learn how to read a racetrack and handle a racing machine. He toured the country spreading the word about highway safety to high-school students and he visited troops in Vietnam. His education began with the rough-and-tumble midgets that competed on the West Coast during an unforgettable period of racing, and it continued as he tried to make his way in the big time on the nation's championship racing circuit.

To illustrate the high level of competition Rodger experienced in his early years: look at the racers who competed on the United Racing Association (URA) and American Automobile Association (AAA) midget circuits and later became the top racers on the championship trail. Consider Bill Vukovich, Sam Hanks, Rex Mays, Tony Bettenhausen, Johnnie Parsons, Jack McGrath, Walt Faulkner, Jimmy Bryan, Troy Ruttman, and Duane Carter to name just a handful.

One fact that cannot be overlooked about Rodger's career is that he literally survived what may have been the most deadly period of racing in America. Hundreds of racing drivers are mentioned in these chapters, but too few of them lived to walk away from the sport. How did he manage to avoid the carnage? Rodger had very few wrecks. In fact, while driving roadsters for A. J. Watson, he only made wall contact twice. And through the course of researching this book, I can only recall two times in more than 20 years of competition when he got upside down in a racing car.

Many consider the years between World War II and the introduction of rear engine cars to the national championship to be America's golden age of racing. It wasn't as complicated then. The drivers started at their local racetracks, earned each step up the ladder, and brought many enthusiastic fans with them. When cars like the legendary *Basement Bessie* competed year after year, it was because of many hours of hard, hands-on labor, and dedication to the sport. Fans recognized that, and mechanics like Watson, Clay Smith, and Ray Nichels earned their own special niches. Just one more reason why going to the races was special during this era.

This effort is dedicated to all of the men who raced because it was fun, because they found their lives too dull when they weren't racing, and because they were good at it. They risked everything without the motivation of bigger sponsorships, more endorsements, or public relations.

Prologue
Dinner in El Paso

In February 1959, a notice in the El Paso evening newspaper reported that colorful racing driver Rodger Ward would be visiting the city to speak at the local high schools as part of the Champion Spark Plugs Highway Safety program. The article caught the attention of a young Air Force enlisted man stationed at the nearby Strategic Air Command base. A clerk in the office of the Director of Material for the 95th Bomb Wing, Larry Wright privately wondered what it would be like to meet Ward, or if it would even be possible.

Hailing from southern Indiana, Larry was familiar with Ward, a top midget and stock car racer who had been competing on the national championship circuit. He broached the subject with one of the sergeants for whom he worked. The sergeant wasn't a racing fan and had never even heard of Ward, yet he assured the young airman that he had nothing to lose and suggested he should try to contact the racing star.

Nervously, Larry phoned the best hotel in El Paso on the day Ward was to arrive. The operator connected him with Ward's room and when Rodger answered the phone, Larry explained that he was a racing fan and would like to meet him.

"He said sure we can get together and I asked what would be a good night, and he said Thursday night—I think it was. He was very agreeable to the idea, and I asked if we could have dinner and just talk, and he said sure. It turned out to be a very pleasant evening; we weren't hurried at all. He was just as comfortable as your next door neighbor," Larry said.

"I'm sure that he knew that he had somebody on the string who was kind of awe inspired at the fact that he was a race driver and I was a fan. At that time I had seen every race since 1946 at Indy, so he knew that I had a little bit of sense going about it."

He recalls that he picked Ward up at the hotel and they took Larry's wife to choir practice at church before going to dinner. "It wasn't out of the way or anything, but I thought it was a little homey for him. [For dinner] we picked an upscale Mexican place. El Paso had a couple of restaurants that were operated by Ashley Gardens. They had a very nice garden atmosphere, a canopy table, and plantings all over the place.

"He was very confident, even in the very early months of the year. The conversation consisted of different elements. We talked about a lot of the fellows that raced and I asked him what he thought of Tony Bettenhausen and he said, 'I wish the old fart would quit.' I think he was fond of him in general and had true feelings for him.

"I had an interest in Dempsey Wilson, because he had signed up to drive Lou Welch's Novi. And of course they had problems those two years he was assigned to the car, and poor Dempsey had to wear the thing practically. And I asked Rodger what he thought about that and he said, 'I'm glad it's him and not me. I wouldn't touch that car with a 10-foot pole.' So he was very real.

"He wasn't over-dressed," Wright continues. "But he had on a shirt and tie. I was impressed with the idea that he could have ordered a drink or two and he didn't, because at that time, people were talking about that about him.

"I kind of wanted to buy just because I wanted to be able to say I bought Rodger Ward dinner. But of course he picked up the check and said, 'No, I'm on an expense account these days and they expect these things.' I was dirt poor in those days and it didn't really matter that much." After dinner, they drove over to the Air Force base and, from the road, Rodger could see the bombers parked outside the hangers.

"As the evening closed, I wanted to get his autograph and I had a Clymer yearbook from the previous year. Rodger was willing to sign the book but he said, 'Can you turn it to the page where the Borg-Warner Trophy is?' That's where he put his autograph, saying, 'I'm going to win that sucker.'"

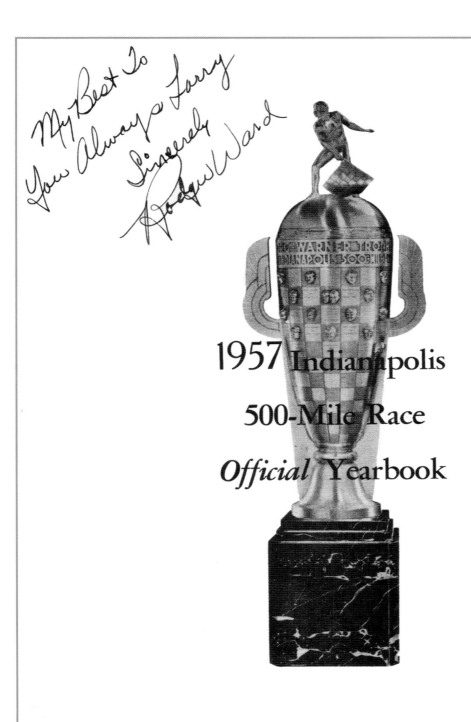

My Best To You Always Larry
Sincerely
Rodger Ward

1957 Indianapolis

500-Mile Race

Official Yearbook

Copyright 1958

by

FLOYD CLYMER

World's Largest Publisher of Books Relating to Automobiles, Motorcycles, Motor Racing, and Americana

1268 SOUTH ALVARADO STREET, LOS ANGELES 6, CALIFORNIA

The page from Larry Wright's *Floyd Clymer's Indianapolis 500 Mile Race Yearbook* that Rodger autographed in 1959. *Larry Wright*

Taken about 1930, this photograph shows Geneva and Ralph Ward's family in Los Angeles. From left to right are children Dorothy, Rodger, Ronnie, and Margaret.
Rodger Ward Jr.

Chapter 1

The Early Years

After Rodger Ward passed away on July 5, 2004, hundreds jammed the San Diego Automotive Museum in Balboa Park to pay tribute to one of motorsport's legends. Rodger had earned the right to be called a legend. His accomplishments were well documented, as friends and racing people were quick to recall.

But like other legends, Rodger was basically just a man trying to make it through the life journey on which he found himself. Even though he had won the Indy 500 twice, beaten the Offys at Gilmore, competed in the Race of Two Worlds, outrun bigger and more powerful sports cars on a road course while driving a midget, was elected to the International Motorsports Hall of Fame, and had been seen as one of racing's most visible ambassadors, in his day-to-day life Rodger confronted the same challenges we all face.

He aspired to a life in the fast lane. In Rodger's case, the timing was right and his success in a glamorous sport allowed

The birth certificate for Rodger Morris Ward, born January 10, 1921. Although his sisters maintain he was born in Colorado, the state of Kansas proves it can claim this two-time Indy winner. *Rodger Ward Jr.*

him to live a lifestyle that was beyond his wildest dreams. As it has been for others, this success proved both a blessing and a curse. He was popular, good looking, well dressed, and a captivating speaker; in general, he exhibited an aura of adventure and excitement. He liked to party until the sun came up and generally found no shortage of willing participants.

At the same time he called himself a loner, as he made no attempt to fit into the conventional factions that filled the pits and garages. He married and was divorced several times. This gave him a reputation as a playboy, perhaps unreliable, and someone who was less than serious about driving racing cars.

At times this reputation was well deserved. Some say Rodger had a dark side, and it contributed to several incidents that profoundly marked his life. There is no doubt his career was hurt by his lifestyle and occasionally by his attitude.

First settled by A. A. Bell in 1868, the town of Beloit sits at the junction of the Union Pacific and Missouri Pacific railroads, along the Solomon River in north central Kansas, 170 miles northwest of Topeka. In that town, Rodger Morris Ward was born to Ralph Arch Ward and Geneva Gertrude (Waters) Ward on January 10, 1921. However, Rodger's older sisters, Dorothy and Margaret, have insisted that Rodger entered the world on the other side of the border in Longmont, Colorado, nearly 500 miles away. Ralph, an auto mechanic by trade, moved the family several times, possibly looking for better work opportunities, at one point to Longmont and eventually to Los Angeles.

In Dick Wallen's book, *Distant Thunder: When Midgets Were Mighty* (2001), author Greg Sharp labels the burgeoning area surrounding Los Angeles a "crucible of speed." Indeed, the crucible in which many motorsports movements were conceived was already forming when the Wards arrived. An exceptional mechanic, Ralph opened Wards Automotive, an auto parts supply and wrecking yard on York Boulevard in Huntington Beach. It wasn't unexpected that Rodger showed an interest in automobiles in his formative years. He was a regular in the wrecking yard at age 12, and it has been noted that he had built a "Ford hot rod" from junkyard parts before he was 14. However, as Rodger Ward Jr. points out, "He built more than one car from spare parts."

Rodger once recalled going to the races as a youngster. "It was at the original Legion Ascot Speedway. All I had to do was walk up over the hill. They raced on Saturday nights, and I'd go over there Saturday afternoons. I could get into the grandstands Saturday afternoon. Then they would throw me out. Then I'd go up on the side of the hill and watch the races."

For a while, Rodger's mother (who had a law degree from a university in Kansas) was the chairperson for the Gideons Women's Auxiliary in Southern California. Rodger Jr. describes his grandmother as "the worst cook in seven states, but she could feed hundreds and do it well. She was a busy missionary for Jesus." In the late 1940s, Ralph and Geneva started a church called the Royal Oaks Community Chapel in Duarte, California. After winning the Indianapolis 500 in 1959, Rodger and his wife at the time, Josephine, contributed financially to the building of this facility.

More interested in hot rods and street racing in Los Angeles than he was in schoolwork, Rodger was spending his time in his father's parts business, working on cars and dreaming of one day becoming a racing driver, when the country went to war. Prior to enlisting, he completed an intense course of study at Creighton University in order to qualify for pilot training. On July 9, 1943, Rodger joined the U.S. Army Air Corps and, in December of the next year, received his advanced single-engine pilot's certificate at Luke Field in Phoenix. He flew P-38 Lightning fighters and, more than once, the turbojet Martin B-51 light bomber. At one time he was reprimanded for strafing whales in the Aleutians.

The P-38 became one of the workhorses in the war effort and as quickly as Lockheed built them, young pilots were needed to fly them. Rodger explained what happened: "I had a little time in a P-38, but the truth of the matter is I had 13 to 15 hours and I thought I was all set to go. I went through gunnery practice and everything, and thought I was going to kill them all. Then my commanding officer called me in and said, 'Lieutenant Ward, we have determined that because you're as good an instrument pilot as we've seen, we're going to make you into an instructor.' So I headed to Luke Air Force Base in Phoenix and instructed all these kids who were coming up."

Sheppard Field, just outside Wichita Falls, Texas, trained the Air Corps' aviation mechanics, engineers for B-29s, and also conducted advanced pilot training. Rodger's next stop was at Sheppard Field, where he was assigned to instructor duty, administering instrument check flights in AT-6s.

Rodger had married Wilma Doris Watson in 1941 and their son, Charles Rodger—more casually known as Rodger Jr.—was born in November. While Rodger was in the Air Corps, the rest of the family stayed in California, and a second son, David Gary Ward, was born in 1945.

Taken at Luke Field in 1944, Lieutenant Ward has just completed pilot training. *Rodger Ward Jr.*

Ernie and Rodger—Part One

In the postwar heyday of California's midgets, Ernie Casale was a successful team owner as well as a top mechanic. In 1953, Casale hired Rodger to drive M. A. Walker's new Kurtis, both at Indianapolis and on the national circuit. For the next three seasons, Ward was Casale's midget chauffeur as they towed the midget and champ cars to AAA races around the country. Following in his father's footsteps, Ernie's son Andy also fielded midgets and today, although more than 70 years old, competes an Offy-powered midget at vintage events. Here's one of a few stories Andy Casale shared about Rodger and his father.

"We were running the blue circuit with our two cars and my dad's two full-time drivers, Billy Cantrell and Bill Zaring. There was a guy, Cecil Shaw, who had the No. 42 Offy that Johnny Garrett was driving. He was a contractor. My dad had been doing a bunch of work for him on his quick-change rear end, hubs, and Offy engine. He got to owing my dad a few bucks. At mid-season or so, he said, 'Ernie, I can't pay you right now, business isn't real good. But why don't you take my car and run it as your third car for the rest of the season.'

"My dad had wanted Rodger to drive, and he and my dad got together and my dad said, 'Rodger I'd like to offer you the ride.'

"He knew the car; it was white and dark maroon. Rodger said, 'I just hate those colors.'

"When my dad got the car from Shaw, he brought it over, and Rodger said, 'Let's strip that paint off and paint it blue and white, just like the rest of the Casale cars.'

"So yours truly and Rodger stripped all the paint off of it with the paint stripper that they had those days. You let it bubble and you'd use a scraper to scrape it off, and then a wire brush to wire-brush it off the aluminum, and be careful not to get it in your eyes; it would burn, it was like acid.

"We got it all stripped out in a couple of days. Rodger had had a paint shop at one time, so he went and got all of the zinc chromate primer and the blue and white, and he started doing all of the painting in my dad's backyard. Then he masked it out and made it two-tone. It was a real nice job. I think this was like on a Monday and they wanted to run at Gilmore on Thursday night. In the meantime, my dad was working on the engine, getting everything ready, besides the other two cars that were already going to run.

"On Wednesday night, Rodger went to Balboa Stadium in San Diego. That night, Rodger crashed and broke his shoulder. Rodger never got to drive the car. My dad had it all ready to go and he put Johnny Garrett back in the car. So Johnny Garrett kind of lost his ride and gained his ride before Rodger ever got to touch it. Rodger never did drive that car. Garrett drove it like six weeks and then my dad gave it back to Shaw. He had made his money out of it.

"Poor Rodger didn't hook up that time, but later on my dad had him drive at the Indianapolis 500."

The Wichita Falls Speedrome was a quarter-mile dirt oval that opened in April 1946. It was built and operated by Abe Rabin and two others, who were in the used car business. As they were in need of additional cars, they purchased a Ford-powered midget and another that employed a Willys-Jeep engine. Rodger talked his way into a job as a mechanic, preparing the midgets for the weekly racing program. But when one of the drivers didn't show up one night, Rodger became a racing driver, too.

"On my first night out," he recalled several years ago, "one of my teammates bumped me and spun me out, and my other teammate came around and bopped me. The windshield jumped up and I got a pretty good cut on my chin. I've still got a good scar there.

"They took me to the hospital and sewed me up. My commanding officer was one of those who could read. I stayed out of everybody's way for a little while. Then finally I went out to race again. [The local newspaper] decided that they would do a little story on 'Lieutenant Rodger Ward being at the races tonight, come out and see!'

"My commanding officer read the newspaper and called me in for a little discussion. He said, 'I don't think hanging around that racetrack out there is a good pastime for an officer and gentleman in the United States Air Corps. I suggest you get out or give it up.' I thought about it for a little while and decided 'what the hell,' and I got out." With the war over and the military in the midst of standing down, Rodger received his discharge on August 18, 1946.

Rodger had made some changes to the midget, installing a shortened Model-T front axle and an in-and-out gearbox. The owners gave him a jeep, trailer to tow the racer, and a budget of new front and rear tires for the right side each week. In perhaps one of his first bits of press, the September 15, 1946, issue of the *Oklahoman* includes Rodger in a summary of the midget competition at Oklahoma City's Taft Stadium. It reports that he participated in one racing program and had apparently won a heat race.

After traveling to Amarillo, Oklahoma City, and Tulsa, Rodger remained in Texas for another month, racing three nights a week. But, as he later noted, Wilma was still in California, with both Rodger Jr. and David, and she gave him the following advice, "You bum. Come home and get a job."

Rodger left Texas and returned to California, where instead of looking for employment, he immediately began to harass everybody he could find in the racing business. His tactics worked. "I got a ride almost right away. I bragged about how great I was in Texas. Nobody believed me and I couldn't prove it to them. But I did get rides."

Rodger focused his efforts on the busy midget contingent around Los Angeles, but also picked up a ride for two roadster races. The roadster didn't run very well in its first outing at Carrell Speedway. But in his second event, at a quarter-mile in Huntington Beach, whatever had been wrong was now right and Rodger was the fastest qualifier, won the trophy dash, finished second in the heat race, and dominated the main event.

Rodger would drive more roadsters to victory, on much more prestigious tracks, later in his career. But first he needed to establish himself in midgets. Which is exactly what he set out to do.

Above: Posing with a BT-15 Vultee Valiant, Rodger is a proud Air Corps pilot instructor. More than 11,000 Vultee Valiants were produced between 1940 and 1944, making it the most prolific basic trainer built during World War II. *Rodger Ward Jr.*

At the wheel of Perry Grimm's Ford-powered car (No. 77), Rodger is just a second away from being slammed by Jimmy Bryan at Balboa Stadium in 1949. *Dick Wallen Collection*

Chapter 2

Glory Days for Midget Racers

When World War II ended in August 1945, California's midget racers were among the first to begin fitting the pieces of life as it used to be back into place. There had been a surprisingly early, and temporary, lift on the racing ban the previous November, and Duke Nalon had won a midget feature at the Indianapolis Speedrome. Then the ban was quickly reinstituted.

Once the ban was officially canceled, West Coast racing was quickly back in full swing with the leadership of United Midget Association's (UMA) Roy Morrison and Roscoe Turner, who were joined by Ray Lavely and Gordon Schroeder. Fresno's Bill Vukovich claimed the first event, at Bonelli Stadium in Los Angeles' Soledad Canyon on September 9, in front of 9,000 paying fans.

World War II triggered tremendous growth in the nation's aircraft industry, and no place was busier than Southern California. The nation, ready to forget wartime life with its

Gilmore Stadium

Today, the origin of Gilmore Stadium reads like a fairy tale. In 1880, A. F. Gilmore and his partner, Julius Carter, dissolved their arrangement by drawing straws to determine who would take which of their two farms. Gilmore's straw claimed a successful 256-acre farm at 3rd and Fairfax in L.A. When he drilled a new well for the water to expand the dairy business, instead of water, he found oil.

Gilmore Oil Company became the largest distributor of petroleum products in the western United States. A. F.'s son, Earl B. Gilmore, is said to have invented self-service gas stations with his Gas-A-Teria, where customers could save a nickel a gallon by pumping their own fuel. Gilmore Blu-Green and Red Lion gas became household names. The Gilmore lion cub became world famous as co-pilot of the Gilmore airplane that set national air speed records in the 1920s and 1930s.

A huge fan of motorsports, Earl Gilmore sponsored Indy 500—winning efforts for Kelly Petillo and Wilbur Shaw. Gilmore Stadium, built on Beverly Boulevard in 1934, was the first venue constructed specifically for the busy emerging midget racing scene.

defense work and rationing, embraced the racing. Big crowds became the norm and soon the midgets were competing six and seven nights a week. The UMA renamed itself the United Racing Association (URA). Tracks included the Los Angeles Memorial Coliseum; Rose Bowl, Culver City; county fairgrounds in Santa Maria (Santa Barbara) and San Joaquin (Stockton); the Bakersfield Speedbowl; Seals Stadium in San Francisco; Airport Speedway in Fresno; Sacramento's Hughes Stadium; and San Jose Speedway.

With the large contingent of sailors and marines stationed nearby, San Diego's Balboa Stadium welcomed 25,000 fans when it re-opened in September. When the L.A. Coliseum hosted its first postwar program, 55,000 spectators watched the action on the quarter-mile asphalt oval fabricated inside. Top drivers and car owners, like the Air Corps' Rex Mays, Sam Hanks, Swede Lindskog, Edgar Elder (who built his first midget when only 16

years old), and Gib Lilly, the Navy's Johnny Pawl, and soldier Jerry Piper were being released from their military duties and returning to the racetracks.

By 1946, the Rose Bowl was regularly counting 20,000 fans. Bonelli opened with 9,000 in April. Newly constructed south of Los Angeles, the Gardena Bowl held its first race on Labor Day weekend and reported attendance of 12,000. At the Coliseum's 250-lap race on August 17th, 65,000 saw Johnnie Parsons collect the victory.

But racing wasn't limited to the West Coast. Chicago's Soldier Field hosted 30,000 in October 1946. While Soldier Field and Blue Island's Raceway Park hosted weekly events, Lou Scally, Marty Wiswald, and Wally Novak formed the United Auto Racing Association (UARA), which competed at Chicago's Hanson Park Stadium during 1947, its inaugural season. Other busy Midwest venues included Detroit's Motor City Speedway, Walsh Stadium in St. Louis, the dirt quarter-mile inside the Milwaukee Fairground oval, Indianapolis' 16th Street Speedway, South Bend Speedway, and the Crown Point Midget Track in Indiana.

Midget racing also boomed in the Pacific Northwest with drivers like Seattle's Allan Heath, Bob Gregg, Louie Sherman, Don Olds, and Shorty Templeman. On the East Coast, Thompson Speedway, West Haven Speedway and Cherry Park racetrack in Connecticut, Freeport Speedway in New York, and Century Stadium in West Springfield, Massachusetts, were among the tracks that were holding regular midget races.

The tube-frame Kurtis-Kraft became the racing machine of choice. A mechanic at Don Lee Cadillac, Frank Kurtis was known for his sheetmetal work. Kurtis began building midgets out of his house in the mid-1930s. By 1941, his shop had built its first Indy car. Supporting the war effort, he switched to building aircraft parts and children's toys. Kurtis' postwar midget was so popular that he established an assembly line, producing 550 complete racers and exceeding that in the number of kits produced. Other cars included the Solar, a postwar product with a steel rail frame that provided a more economical approach to racing.

Today, the Offenhauser powerplant has become legendary. Offys were first developed for big car competition, but in the late-1930s the first eight-valve double-overhead cam (DOHC) four-cylinder midget engine was fabricated. With 94 ci, it produced 120 horsepower. When combined with a Kurtis chassis, the package was the best available.

Fresno's Bill Vukovich was one of California's top midget stars. He reached national fame, winning the Indianapolis 500 twice in the 1950s. *Don Radbruch Collection*

Close racing action at Gilmore Stadium sometimes included acrobatics. Bill Homeier's ride over Bobby Ball's nose is a classic. *Don Radbruch Collection*

Johnnie Parsons, seen here with a Drake-powered car, was another of the prewar midget veterans who drew large crowds to AAA races. After winning Indy in 1950, he continued racing until he retired in 1958. *Don Radbruch Collection*

Sam Hanks cut his teeth racing midgets before the War. He retired in Victory Lane at Indianapolis in 1957. *Don Radbruch Collection*

A money-saving alternative was the little Drake engine, which was developed by Dale and Lem Drake. Based on the bottom end of a Harley Davidson V-twin, it weighed 185 pounds and displaced 89 ci. Although smaller and developing less horsepower than the Offy, many found it effective. Vukovich was just one of the racing stars who found a lot of success with the Drake.

Ford's V8-60 contained 136 ci and was approximately two-thirds the size and horsepower of its flathead V-8. Its 60 horses were half that of the Offy, but the reduced price made it appealing. Although only produced between 1937 and 1941, enough found their way into midgets to leave their mark.

As a national organization, AAA was slower to organize racing on a local level, its focus being on the national championship events and, in particular, the Indianapolis 500. Other than AAA, the URA was clearly the biggest midget group in the country. Based in California and taking advantage of the postwar popularity, the URA was organized into two complementary series, called the Blue and Red Circuits. The most obvious difference between the two is the Blue Circuit featured Offy-powered midgets, while the Red Circuit hosted a variety of powerplants, including Fords and Drakes.

Interestingly, significant geographic and even cultural variations grew out of this arrangement. Dick Wallen's book, *Distant Thunder When Midgets Were Mighty* (2001), accurately characterizes the distinctions between the groups and their fans. The Blue Circuit was best known for drivers in bright satin shirts competing at Gilmore, the Coliseum, and Legion Ascot, while heading to Bonelli was considered "a long drive out to the sticks to see second-rate cars driven by guys in T-shirts."

To the racers, however, both were good paydays and the racing was top-notch. Bill Vukovich was the champion of the Red Circuit in both 1945 and 1946 in his red Drake-powered car; on the Blue Circuit, Mel Hansen and Hanks earned the titles. Many of the top drivers regularly competed in both circuits and frequently had to choose between opposing events on the same day. Occasionally, they were able to organize their transportation and resources to race in both events on the same day.

The purse racers competed for was a percentage of what the tracks collected at the admission gates. Even though most organizers and track officials did a good job keeping an accurate, documented count of attendance and receipts, there were occasional problems. However, knowing that if the fans got a

Young and good looking, Rodger knew how to take full advantage of being a midget star. *Don Radbruch Collection*

good show they were likely to keep coming back became an overriding factor for nearly everyone involved.

In terms of enduring popularity, the biggest venue of all was Gilmore Stadium, with Hollywood stars in the grandstand and the traditional Thanksgiving Day Gilmore Grand Prix. The quickly arranged 1945 Grand Prix, although held on a Tuesday night and shortened to 75 laps, was won by "Dapper" Danny Oakes in front of a capacity crowd of more than 18,000. With its unique touches—like the one-of-a-kind scoreboard, twin timepieces, Hollywood luminaries, and uniformed ushers—Gilmore established Thursday nights as its own territory in the racing world.

In addition to the location and unique character of Gilmore Stadium, its appeal was the result of close and exciting racing. The Gilmore's track surface was comprised of a mixture of decomposed granite and adobe-like clay, allowing tremendous grip from the midget tires. The turns were slightly banked, allowing the drivers to run fast on either the bottom or farther up the tracks in the turns. Given the right conditions and setup,

Rodger spins in Lysle Greenman's midget (No. 35) as Frank Armi, Danny Oakes, Edgar Elder, and Bill Vukovich race past. Vuky, in Fred Gerhardt's 45, is looking to see if Ward will keep going. *Lee Harvey photo, Roy C. Morris Collection*

a driver could really hook up at the top of the banking. Although a longer route around the oval, the car would carry a higher rate of speed through the turns and more momentum onto the straightaway than one running the inside groove.

Unlike Gilmore, other tracks of the day usually became hard and slick. Drivers who cut their teeth in that environment learned to race aggressively and with a high degree of car control. The number of drivers who raced in California's URA and AAA midget circuits during the postwar boom and then went on to national prominence easily demonstrated the level of competition in midget racing.

The legendary "Vuky" Vukovich may have been the greatest driver of that generation. After the war, he made a steady living on the Red Circuit, where in addition to his 1945 and 1946 championships, he finished second to Bill Cantrell in 1947. Moving to the Blue Circuit in 1948 with his car owner and buddy from Fresno, Fred Gerhardt, Vukovich was third in the standings, behind L.A.'s Bill Zaring and Norman Gritz, and also captured Gilmore's Thanksgiving Grand Prix.

In 1949, Vuky and Gerhardt took on AAA and Vuky finished the season fifth in points, then captured the national AAA midget title the next year. Just two seasons later, Vukovich stood the Indianapolis 500 on its ear when he led almost the whole race, and only missed winning when a steering piece failed with two laps to go. In 1953 and 1954 he was unstoppable, becoming only the third back-to-back winner at Indy.

Rodger in Greenman's midget in 1948. He would race for Lysle again years later at Indy. *Rodger Ward Jr.*

Troy Ruttman, whose first races came in California's roadsters, was quickly in demand in the midgets. Young and brave, Ruttman also proved to be fast and capable, winning the Blue Circuit championship in 1948. The next year, J. C. "Aggie" Agajanian hired Ruttman to pilot one of his AAA cars, but let him go just as quickly when it came to light he wasn't even 20 years old yet. Driving for others, Ruttman was third in AAA midget standings at the end of the season. Rejoining Aggie, Ruttman captured both the Midwest and West Coast AAA sprint car titles in 1951 and, in 1952, won Indy, and ran second in the national championship in addition to repeating the Midwest sprint title.

Another of the era's top runners, Johnnie Parsons had been the UMA champion in 1942, the last season before racing was halted for the war. He was the 1948 AAA Midwest midget champion and became United States Auto Club's (USAC) Pacific Coast champ in 1956. Moving to the national championship's

big cars in 1949, he earned that title, then won the Indy 500 the following May.

The story continues with Sam Hanks, the URA's 1946 Blue Circuit champion, who had claimed the American Midget Association (AMA) crown in 1937. Twenty years after winning the AMA championship, Hanks retired in victory lane at Indianapolis. Another driver who would go on to make a name for himself was the young Jimmy Bryan, who traveled from Phoenix with Bobby Ball to run California's midgets in 1948. Bryan's raw talent was such that he scored 10 URA wins and was fifth in 1949 Blue Circuit standings. He advanced to fourth the next year, while the lanky Ball claimed third in the 1950 AAA West Coast midget points. Like Vukovich, Ruttman, Parsons,

Dad's Burns

Although just a toddler at the time, Rodger Jr. remembers his father received some nasty burns early in his career. "My dad and mom were divorced and he was away quite a bit when I was an infant. I remember his accident when he got burned at Saugus. In his very first car race, in Texas, is where he got that scar that he wore on his chin all his life. I remember him coming home from being burned—and I guess that water boiled over on him—and the doctor had given him sulfa and he was allergic to it. My father had an unmatchable threshold of pain. Think about those little nicks and notches that he had on his arms [from racing in the open cockpit cars]. He had a real high tolerance for pain. You'd never hear him say 'ouch' or 'dammit.' If he cut himself, he'd throw a piece of masking tape, or any kind of tape, around it and just keep on going. It didn't bother him—and in places where we are sensitive to cuts and bruises.

"Because he was burned in a race car, he toughed that out. But when that sulfa started itching, now he was broken out in itching hives all over his body, underneath itching blisters from the hot liquid that managed to spew out all over him. About that, he bitched."

and Hanks, Bryan was among the veterans of the postwar midgets to win at the Brickyard in the 1950s.

In fact, for several generations many of the top drivers came up through the midgets. Among them were Walt Faulkner, Paul Russo, Duane Carter, Mel Hansen, Johnny Mantz, Colorado's Johnny Tolan, Len Sutton from Portland, Freddie Agabashian, Andy Linden, Manny Ayulo, and Bob Swanson. Additionally, some of the best midget racers gained tremendous regional popularity, although like New York's Bill Schindler, they earned little of the national spotlight. Ed Haddad, Danny Oakes, Allen Heath, Chick Barbo, L.A.'s burly Perry Grimm, Karl Young, and Eli, Vuky's brother, were among the most popular West Coast midget racers, yet they garnered little national attention.

The top drivers were in great demand. The AAA was trying to hold its own as regional racing groups started popping up around the country. One of the ploys the AAA used was to require its drivers only compete in AAA-sanctioned events. This meant that if a driver had the desire to race at Indianapolis or for the national championship, he would have to skip the busy URA Blue and Red circuits and limit his midget racing to the less-frequent AAA events or face a suspension. In 1947, the URA ran 331 races, while the AAA only mustered 43 midget events. The result was tremendous competition to secure the drivers and cars, not only between the two organizations, but also for every race

Rodger Makes the Scene

It was at the peak of this era that 26-year-old Rodger Ward headed home to join California's midget scene. He didn't have a regular ride, but raced wherever opportunities arose. With his fighter-pilot background, he found he easily fit into the racing environment. He worked hard and he made mistakes, but that went with being a young gun quickly learning to hold his own in the rough-and-tumble world of midget racing, where most tracks were small and fast and racing was literally wheel-to-wheel. In addition to midgets, he ran a couple of roadster events and even drove a Jeep in a 250-mile stock car race at Carrell Stadium on October 4, as the 1947 racing season began to wrap up.

Rodger Jr. recalls that, while paying his racing dues, his father would go to Clovis and pick lettuce to make money between races. Wilma told Rodger he needed to come home and get a job. "That was the time when I told him it wasn't going to be working out for us," she recalled. "He didn't want a job; he wanted to drive race cars."

Rodger's first midget win came in the Red Circuit's Grand Prix at Balboa Stadium on November 26, 1947. Driving the No. 63 West V8-60 Ford, he took the lead when Johnny Mantz's car broke, then held off Walt Faulkner in the closing laps. Rodger completed the 100-lap race in a record time of 30 minutes, 12.36 seconds, and claimed the largest share of the $3,400 purse. When the season ended, Rodger had earned 101 Blue Circuit points and finished 18th in the final standings.

Lysle Greenman—Different from other Subs

His victory at Balboa caught the right kind of attention. Lysle Greenman, a prominent L.A. Chrysler-Plymouth dealer, was putting together a two-car team for the 1948 season, and Perry Grimm suggested that the mechanic for Greenman's race team, Bill Mathews, go to San Diego and watch a young driver named Ward. Mathews, who was once known as William Max Albert

Feja, had won several races at the wheel of a Frontenac in the late 1920s. He was impressed by what he saw and hired Rodger, commenting on his smoothness. Ward was assigned Greenman's No. 35 Offy and began the season on the right foot, winning the Blue Circuit's fifth outing, a 50-lapper at Bonelli Stadium on April 4.

In Gilmore Stadium's May 6 opener, Faulkner and Bobby Ball made contact, with Faulkner flipping and landing on Ward's tail. But that was just a temporary setback, as Rodger claimed six additional wins during the year: June 18 at San Bernardino, 50 laps; July 9 at San Bernardino, 30 laps; July 29 at Gilmore, 60 laps; September 4 at Carpinteria, 50 laps; September 6 at Balboa, 75 laps; and September 25 at San Bernardino, 50 laps. All were Blue Circuit events except the big Labor Day show at Balboa, where he wheeled the No. 65 Ford V8-60 owned by Perry Grimm.

"We raced six or seven nights a week," Rodger Jr. recalls. Even though it was certain to cut into his social life, the father would take his boy to the races. "So every now and then, he'd pick me up and I'd go with him. I had to be a terrible pain in the ass, from his perspective. Because, you know, what he was used to doing is going to the racetrack, showing off with his little helmet, doing a little of this and that, and going home with the trophy girl. And now he had his little son with him. And we'd go and race Fresno on Friday night, Bakersfield on Saturday night, and go back to Fresno on Sunday afternoon. I went to a lot of races with him like that. He was always my hero. I still say, 'Let's blow this pop stand!' and that was something that I got from him. My dad always had the hippest lingo."

In between chasing trophy girls, Rodger joined in matrimony a carhop named Nikki. It was another case of true love. Short-lived true love, however, as Rodger's priority was his racing career.

Although Rodger captured seven URA wins during the 1948 season, Greenman's other car, No. 25, won just twice—with Don Cameron at Bakersfield in April and Allen Heath at Carpinteria in August. Frustrated by the overall lack of success, Greenman completely reorganized for the 1949 campaign, losing Rodger in the process.

Despite the close competition, traveling and racing together several times each week for the majority of the year led to strong bonds between the racers. On the road in the days before interstate travel and convenient airline service—and certainly before lucrative contracts—drivers frequently shared rides and

The Edelbrock Connection

A native of Los Angeles, Vic Edelbrock had taken his 1932 Ford roadster to the Muroc Dry Lake where he reached more than 120 miles per hour just weeks before Pearl Harbor. After the war, Edelbrock opened a machine shop in Hollywood and was soon specializing in aluminum cylinder heads for flat-head Ford racing engines. With the resurgence of the powerful little machines, he bought a car that had been built by D. W. McCully. Before the end of 1946, Edelbrock—a midget owner prior to the war—had purchased one of the earliest midgets built in Frank Kurtis' shop.

He soon had a two-car team running as many as six times each week. The red-and-cream Kurtis-Krafts, carrying Ford V8-60s, were among the strongest cars on either circuit, and Edelbrock employed top drivers like San Bernardino's Oakes, Faulkner, Grimm, Heath, and Mack Hellings. In 1947, he added a highly competitive Offy. Perry Grimm won several races, but since Vic was selling Ford racing equipment, the success of the Offy wasn't helping business.

According to Buzz Rose, a subsequent owner of the 1946 Ford-powered Kurtis, the latter had a spring suspension while the 1947 Kurtis, outfitted with the Offy, had torsion bars. At the end of the season, Edelbrock asked Grimm which car he should sell, and Grimm said that he liked the "feel" of the car with torsion bars much better. Edelbrock sold the V8-60 Kurtis to Homer Norman in Washington State, and the Offy midget was converted to Ford power.

Vic Edelbrock Jr. was a teenager at the time and recalls, "I was always on the team as far as when I was out of school, I got to wash the car every day after it came back from the races because, running on a clay track, it got pretty dirty. I cleaned the engine up and everything. They'd let me do small things where I wouldn't get in trouble. The midget was always a big part of my life.

"My dad put Rodger to work. He said, 'If you're going to drive, you're going to get yourself together.' And he put him to work in my dad's little facility. And that's where I got to know Rodger. We were burring parts that my dad had made. Because of the Korean War, he had gone back and started making stuff for Lockheed and Northrop. Rodger and I had the job every once in a while of sitting on stools with a little low table between us, and we would very delicately de-burr the castings that were machined and had to be done just right."

Rodger was 15 years older than Vic Jr. It said a lot about his focus at that time. He had been an Air Force officer, a fighter pilot, was an up-and-coming midget star, and divorced by this time with two young kids at home. Yet he chose to spend his days helping a teenager, still in high school, burr parts for an insignificant wage. Vic Jr. says he'll never forget how Rodger spent much of the time entertaining him with stories of nights on the town and explaining how to treat the girls. However, the potential that Vic Sr. saw in the young racer compelled him to retain Rodger as pilot of his No. 27 Kurtis/Ford machine.

accommodations. In addition to respect on the track, the regulars formed long-lasting friendships that endured as they moved up racing's ladder.

Bill Mathews, Ward's crew chief on the Greenman team, decided to field his own Kurtis/Offy with sponsorship from Art Frost De Soto for 1949 and stayed with Ward as the driver. Their first victory came at San Bernardino on June 3. On the 25th, they collected another Blue Circuit win, this time a 40-lap affair at Culver City. Two weeks later, Ward won another Culver City 40-lapper. Then, out of the blue, Mathews parked the car, noting that Rodger was partying too much. The midget would stay in his garage for the next 20 years.

A. J. "Bud" Murphy, a pilot for Trans World Airlines, frequently drove his own No. 6 *Herb and Chucks* Offy, named for the service station on L.A.'s Pico Boulevard where he kept the midget. When Rodger captured a third Culver City win on August 6, this time at the wheel of Murphy's Offy, it would be his last visit to victory lane in 1949.

Vic Edelbrock

Although busy driving for Vic Edelbrock, Perry Grimm had his own Ford-powered midget, which Edelbrock maintained. Grimm put Rodger in that car. One night, Jimmy Bryan tried to pass for third on the last lap at San Diego. Bryan misjudged his

Chief mechanic Bill Mathews hired Rodger to drive one of Lysle Greenman's Offys in 1948. Here, Rodger is ready for the program to start at San Bernardino's Orange Show Stadium. *Dick Wallen Collection*

maneuver and slid into Ward's machine, sending it into a series of violent flips. Rodger was sidelined while his broken right arm and left wrist healed.

When he returned at the end of the season, Edelbrock assigned Rodger to his No. 27 that had been vacated by Grimm. Vic Edelbrock Jr. recalls, "Rodger's first race was at Culver City. He had hurt himself in Perry Grimm's car and hurt his shoulder, so he was out for a while. Now Rodger wasn't much for being idle when he was out; he loved to party and he loved the girls and the whole nine yards. So he was a little bit out of shape and my dad said, 'Drive the midget at Culver City.' It was

the last race of the year. And after 30 laps, they had to lift him out of the car—he couldn't get out."

As quickly as it had blossomed just a handful of years earlier, racing found itself in a rapid downward spiral of poor attendance, low car counts, and shrinking purses. By 1950, the URA's Blue Circuit had been critically weakened by the AAA. While the non-Offy Red Circuit was still pulling healthy car

Rodger won seven main events driving for Lysle Greenman in 1948. *Dick Wallen Collection*

counts, Blue Circuit tracks hoped to survive by running what the URA called "open" events, where a certain number of feature starting spots were held open for the Fords and Drakes. These took place at Gilmore, Balboa in San Diego, San Bernardino's Orange Show Stadium, and the Culver City oval.

Although he had spent a lot of time racing on the Red Circuit, Edelbrock preferred the payoff and competition of the Blue Circuit. For the 1950 season, Vic decided to run his cars at the open tracks with Rodger in No. 27. Vic had installed an early dynamometer in his engine shop, and he and mechanic Bobby Meeks were experimenting with the power output of the Fords. Business was booming and he was selling a lot of powerplants to all kinds of racers looking for more speed, from midget teams to those headed for the desert's dry lakes. Vic needed a driver who could showcase his products by winning, and he liked what he saw in Rodger.

The first win in Rodger's new ride came at the Orange Show Stadium's season-opening event on April 20. On May 4, he scored again at San Bernardino. He moved to the Morrison/Cayer Ford for a Red Circuit win on May 20, then back in the Edelbrock Kurtis, he captured a 30-lap open race at Culver City six days later. June 1950 turned out to be the best month of Rodger's career. Showing they could win at different tracks, Rodger and the Edelbrock team earned consecutive open

event wins at San Diego's Balboa Stadium on the 14th, Culver City on the 16th, San Bernardino on the 22nd, Bakersfield two days later, and returned to Culver City for a win on the 30th. In between, Rodger jumped into the Temple No. 35 Ford, in which Bill Cantrell drove to a pair of victories and Johnny Garrett earned one win, to claim another Red Circuit show at Sacramento on June 19.

"You couldn't drive for Vic Edelbrock and not look like a superstar," Rodger Jr. points out, "because in those days, the race cars worked. You could only adjust them a little bit. Heck, Herb Porter said that he used to weld the settings on his dirt cars and then let the driver be the difference. And the driver could be the difference, in a huge way, much more than now."

Quoting Scripture

"After Rodger was driving my dad's midget all the time and he had already driven the first year for my dad as a crew chief at Indianapolis in 1953, we were getting both his midget and champ cars ready to go race two different venues. My dad used to have the drivers and the crew guys—including myself—come over and he'd feed them, then they'd go out in the garage and work on the cars. So we were sitting around the table one evening and all the guys were coming in to eat. My mom usually made a big plate of rigatoni. So he called all of the guys in and I had to get my homework done because I was still in high school.

"So I was starting to do my homework and grabbing a bite to eat, and Rodger started asking some questions: 'Where do you go to school?'

"I said, 'I go to a Catholic school.'

"And my father said, 'Yeah, Rodger, you probably wouldn't know too much about that religion.'

"And Rodger says, 'What do you mean?' Then Rodger started quoting scripture. He said, 'I know all about the Bible.'

"And he started doing one after the other, after the other. It was really comical, because you wouldn't have expected him to know all of that. But he sure did."

Photographed before the start of the main event at Culver City in 1948, Rodger is already having a good time. Front row, left to right: Bill Cantrell, Ray Crawford, Bill Zaring, Bobby Ball, and Johnny Garrett. Standing or seated in the back row, left to right: Troy Ruttman, Allen Heath, Ward, Tommy Elliott, unknown, Bill Taylor, Bill Homeier, Danny Oakes, and Duane Sears. *Lee Harvey photo, Roy C. Morris Collection*

As the season rolled into summer, Ward and the Edelbrock team had little time to cool off. They were running well enough to pose a threat to win every time the gates opened. They scored hard-fought victories against Offys on consecutive nights, July 12, 13, and 14 in open circuit events at Balboa, San Bernardino, and Culver City.

One of the team's experimental interests was in improvements gained by using fuel additives. Although the use of nitromethane (a rocket fuel), commonly shortened to nitro, to boost power would quickly become more widespread, in 1950 it was virtually unknown.

Short, mustachioed Ed Haddad was instrumental in Edelbrock's introduction to nitro. Haddad had obtained a gallon of the fuel from the Dooling brothers, who used it to power one of the aluminum slot cars that they had built. Edelbrock Jr. clearly remembers that afternoon: "[Haddad] gave it to my dad and said, 'I don't know what the hell to do with this stuff; you might just see if it works.'"

Edelbrock Jr. recalls that they put it in a Ford flathead and ran it on the dyno without adjusting any of the plugs or jetting, resulting in a very lean and very hot mixture. "They saw the scale on the dyno act very favorably, and they went to shut it off and it wouldn't shut off; it was like a glow plug. So they finally threw rags over the carburetor and that got it to stop. They got to looking at things, and things were pretty well fried in there.

"That's when they decided, 'Well, it works. We have to run it and we've got to run more fuel, colder spark plugs, and change a few things.' So that's when they went back to Dooling

Gilmore's Thanksgiving Grand Prix was easily the biggest night of the year. Drivers ready for the racing to start in 1948 include: Back row, left to right: Don Farmer, Jimmy Bryan, Bill Vukovich, Bill Cantrell, Bill Taylor, Perry Grimm, Eli Vukovich, Johnny Garrett, Karl Young. Front row, left to right: Bill Zaring, Danny Oakes, Ward, Ray Crawford, Allen Heath, and Walt Faulkner. *Lee Harvey photo, Rodger Ward Jr. Collection*

brothers and got more fuel. And when they were all through with the V8-60, they could run 20 percent [nitro in the fuel] and they gained 40 percent on the horsepower."

Although at first Vic didn't tell Rodger what their secret was, he did warn him they were running an experimental fuel, so it might have an odd smell and the engine would sound a little different. They added a chemical that masked the nitro by making the exhaust smell like orange peel while also changing the color of the flame to orange. He added that Rodger could expect to be running faster.

Rodger admitted he didn't press Vic for any details. "I said, 'I don't care. As long as the S.O.B. runs, I don't care.' I'll tell you what, I never got beat to the first turn if I started on the front row by any Offenhauser. That S.O.B. was unreal!"

Ironically, their biggest victory would come in the closing days of what many consider a golden period in American motor-

sports. After busy seasons filled with excited crowds, the glitter of Hollywood's most popular stars and starlets, and racing reaching such popularity that some drivers acquired their own celebrity status, Gilmore Stadium was reaching the end of its days. With attendance in decline, in spite of great racing battles (featuring Vukovich, Danny Oakes, Sam Hanks, and other AAA stars), when the top drivers headed to Indianapolis for the May events, the decision was made to suspend racing until later in the summer. Behind the scenes, unknown to most fans, management had begun negotiations with CBS for the sale of Gilmore Stadium.

The End of an Era
In an attempt at boosting car counts to bring fans through the gates, an agreement was reached with the AAA allowing URA teams to compete in AAA races at Gilmore when it reopened.

Bill Zaring in Ernie Casale's Offy and Holtkamp driving for Roscoe Hogan scored wins.

In the nearly five years of racing after the war, there was still one very obvious mountain that had not been scaled. The Offy was still unbeaten at Gilmore. Many of the top drivers and teams had tried, but they had come up short every time.

Rodger Jr. points out that his father was proudest when he was able to physically outrace the other drivers: "When, rather than having the fastest race car, you made it up through determination. But he also proved that he wasn't reckless. He'd go out there and dust it off, dust it off, dust it off, dust it off, dust it off, until everybody thought he was going to try to go high. And then he'd just diamond the prick and drive it right down through all of the holes, trash and ruts and everything like that. A lot of guys who would race down in the holes and ruts and all of that crap were guys who were staying down there and being sort of death-defying. I don't think my dad was a coward by any means, but I don't think he took foolish chances, in sharp contrast to some guys who you see that just do stupid things."

Although this was something Rodger certainly learned in the midgets, it was characteristic of his whole career.

The four-abreast parade thrills fans before the start at Gilmore in July 1949. Bill Cantrell is in the number one on the pole, with Rodger next in Bill Mathews' No. 35 Kurtis-Offy. Also on the front row: Eli Vukovich and Edgar Elder. The second row consists of Bill Zaring in Ernie Casale's No. 9, Allen Heath, Ray Crawford, and PeeWee Distarce. *Lee Harvey photo, Roy C. Morris Collection*

Bobby Meeks and the crew unloaded the red-and-cream-colored Edelbrock Kurtis in Gilmore's pits on August 10, 1950, and immediately things weren't going right. Of the 35 midgets that qualified, Pee Wee Distance set the fastest time at 14.35 seconds in his red No. 25 Offy, followed by Norm Holtcamp, Bobby Ball, and George Amick. At 14.57, Rodger ranked 11th. Lining up for the third heat race, which was inverted based on qualifying times, Rodger started outside of Allen Heath on the front row and trailed him at the finish.

The main event was a 50-lap affair with the third-heat race finishers starting up front, followed by the second heat, then the first, which had the fastest qualifiers. For the second time that night, Heath had the pole in Lysle Greenman's No. 98 with Rodger on his right. It shouldn't have been surprising that the track wasn't in prime condition for racing, which had become a Gilmore tradition. Everyone knew the stadium had been sold and would be bulldozed into oblivion after the summer. Management had already begun to cut corners, and track preparation was minimized. Aggravating the situation were the Santa Ana winds that had blown consistently for several days and only subsided late that afternoon. The result was a hard, dry, shiny, slick surface by the time the drivers lined up for the feature race.

While Rodger had claimed several victories over the best midgets and drivers that summer and was known for winning with spectacular efforts on the cushion that built up outside the groove where most of the drivers raced, this celebrated win would completely contradict that scenario. At the green flag, Heath charged out front with such abandon he slid

Rodger was known for preferring to work in the outside groove. Here, he has the Edelbrock Ford wound up against the Offys of Bud Clemons (14) and Walt Faulkner (15). The No. 14, owned by Ernie Surdo, was an older rail frame midget that competed strongly against the Kurtis-Krafts. *Roy C. Morris Collection*

through the first turn groove and skated high, opening the door for Ward.

While Heath tried to keep his car off the wall, Rodger turned down to the inside lane and began running a controlled and steady pace around the inside of the oval, where there was still a little moisture. As long as he could keep his tires from slipping out toward the middle of the track, anyone who wanted to pass would have to venture up into the hard slick part of the track. However, this wasn't the biggest problem second-running Danny Oakes found. The dose of nitro that had been added to Rodger's fuel was leaving an invisible trail of fumes that made Oakes' eyes burn. For 50 laps, Oakes found it impossible to get close to the Edelbrock Ford, and everyone was nose-to-tail behind him.

Rodger would later relate that Vic and his wife had just returned from a vacation in Hawaii, and he didn't even come to the pits until after the race. Rodger recalled Edelbrock's exhilaration after the race, "He came down; rather, he floated down. 'You don't know what you just did for me!' he said.

"I said, 'And what is that, sir?'

"'I have dreamed about winning a main event at Gilmore Stadium in a Ford and you accomplished that goal!'"

Riding the crest of that excitement, the Edelbrock crew repeated the victory at San Bernardino the next night. This time, the field was just as strong, but the track demanded a superior performance. In retrospect, the San Bernardino win was technically a more impressive feat, but has been largely forgotten in the shadow of Rodger's Gilmore Stadium victory. While using nitro was completely legal, it did not make beating the Offy easy but leveled the playing field for the Ford.

"Gilmore was the premier midget racetrack in the world and to run there against a full field of Offys and win the race was a great, great thrill," Rodger explained many times later in life. Even though he achieved other accomplishments, it was that one race he was asked about again and again.

Vic Edelbrock Jr. had a perfect view of this achievement from inside the pits and garage. "It was the only V8-60 to ever beat the Offys," he explained. "The V8-60 was like a square wheel compared to a round wheel of the Offy. The Offy is a double-overhead cam engine. It has a hemispherical combustion chamber. The V8-60 has a port like the tunnel of love, the exhaust port in it. It never could stand up to running with the Offy unless we had nitromethane in it. That's when it was gaining 40 percent of its power; whatever exactly that was, I don't know. My dad had run an Offy in 1947, along with his V8-60, and they knew what the power of the Offy was on methanol and they knew they had it beat. But the thing was that the V8-

60 in no way could beat the Offy. Then it happened . . . in Gilmore Stadium."

Edelbrock Jr. maintains they were the only ones trying to use nitro, and only had it at the end of the 1950 season. "Rodger won most of those races on methanol. My dad had a few tricks and knew how to make a V8-60 run good just on methanol. It wasn't just the engine, it was also the chassis. We have the car back here and it's all been restored. There are certain things in there that Bobby Meeks showed me that I never knew either, that my dad had done to make the car handle better. You take good handling along with good horsepower and you have a real winner."

With the successes he achieved in the 1950 season, Rodger was ready to move up racing's ladder. However, an incident at

Right: Although his parents were divorced, Rodger Ward Jr. spent considerable time at racetracks while his father raced. He got to know his father as well as anyone. Rodger Jr. once explained, "He was always my hero. I still say, 'Let's blow this pop stand!' and that was something that I got from him. My dad always had the hippest lingo." *Rodger Ward Jr.*

Opposite: Vic Edelbrock didn't go looking for nitro. But when Ed Haddad gave him his first bottle, Vic had the imagination and curiosity to see what would happen if he tried to fire an engine with nitro-spiked fuel. Edelbrock also had the expertise to experiment and make it work before anyone else knew what was happening. *Rodger Ward Jr.*

the end of the season reflects the difficulties that would trouble Rodger for much of the decade.

Vic Jr. recounts, "Rodger was focused on a lot of stuff that wasn't very good for him. The last race he drove for my father was against the Offys at Pomona Fairground and it was an Agajanian promoted program. It was 100 miles. They had enlarged the fuel tank in the midget and had a deal where they pressurized oil so they could turn the nozzle and pump oil into the engine and all of that. Rodger qualified fairly well—I forget exactly where—and I remember watching as the race went on and on. Pretty soon Rodger was in third spot and they thought

maybe he was going to get low on fuel, so the game plan was to bring him in and just splash a little bit of fuel and then send him back out.

"They finally brought him in when he had about 10 or 15 laps to go. They dumped a quick 5 gallons in and so Rodger had to pump fuel pressure with the hand pump. He was so tired that he couldn't work the hand pump. So they pushed him out and the engine tried and tried to run. My father had a mechanical fuel pump on there that would pump air into the tank, so that the driver didn't have to use the hand pump all the time. He went all the way around that mile track and

came back around and they lifted him out and set him on the ground. Billy Cantrell got in and finished the race. But by that time it was back in the middle. It was a lot of money; they had a full house there that day. So my dad found out that Rodger had been partying the night before and didn't get much sleep. That was the problem. Ward was pretty well done anyway because he was going to go back and run at Indy—that was his game plan."

Midget racing continues, more than a half century later. But the period on the West Coast immediately after the war has never been equaled. Racing at different tracks nearly every night of the week, with the top racers in the country, the Offys, the glamour, and the excitement, it was unique.

In the following decades, Edelbrock built a speed empire and his performance products became world famous. He sold the midget (one of several unnumbered Kurtis chassis) that became known as the "Offy Killer" to Frank Pavese, who fielded several top Midwestern drivers including Bob Tattersall. Subsequently, Danny Frye and Mike Riley also owned and raced the car. Today, it has been restored by the Edelbrock family and holds a position of honor in the foyer of the Edelbrock offices in Los Angeles.

In Gasoline Alley, a Firestone tire worker checks the air pressures before Rodger heads out to practice in 1951.

Chapter 3

The Championship Trail

By 1951, World War II, which had profoundly impacted every part of the country, was six years in the past. The nation was quickly moving into a new lifestyle. Rodger's career started taking bigger steps; he had won a dozen times in one of the country's premier series in 1950 alone. He had become somewhat of a star and the rest of the racing world had begun to take notice. The new opportunities he was looking for began to arrive.

The first opportunity came quicker than he expected. Leo Dobry, who ran a salvage yard from a building in downtown Tacoma, Washington, asked him to drive in the national championship event at Phoenix in November of 1950.

Dobry's Offy-powered Kurtis 2000 was known as *Esmeralda* at the time, and it presented a mixed record. Johnnie Parsons had driven it in the previous event at Sacramento. Relegated

Left: Starter Seth Klein, on the left, talks with Rodger shortly before heading out on his qualifying run. *Rodger Ward Jr.*

Right: Two hot dogs! Rodger was one of the top young midget racers coming out of California in 1951. The bulldog is obviously a ham. *IMS Photo*

to shopping for a ride before every race after the team that fielded his Indy 500-winning effort broke up, Parsons dropped out with a broken radius rod and was scored 11th. But in 1948, the Dobry Kurtis, known then as the *City of Tacoma*, had earned a sixth place finish at Indy with Hal Cole at the wheel. At next year's 500, Jack McGrath started it on the front row but fell out early with a failed oil pump.

Rodger started 16th and ran to the checkers on Phoenix's 1-mile dirt oval, where he was awarded 10th after completing 98 laps. Although *Esmeralda* continued to show up for races in the next couple of years, it would rarely make the starting field. Then in 1952, George Hammond won the Pikes Peak Hill Climb in the machine.

1951

For much of the twentieth century, the biggest auto race anywhere was the Indianapolis 500. It was racing's World Series or Super Bowl. Highly respected around the world, many Grand Prix champions competed because they knew their careers wouldn't be complete without adding Indianapolis to their résumé. Its reputation wasn't the result of a well-coordinated professional public relations effort, but rather it was painfully earned by hard work, by tough competition, and literally by

blood, sweat, and tears spent over many decades. It was quite simply the pinnacle of a driver's career.

The majority of the drivers who raced at Indy competed on the AAA's national championship circuit, which was the premier racing series in the country. It consisted of 12 to 14 events on paved and dirt ovals, plus the Pikes Peak Hill Climb.

Rodger began the year driving Lou Bromme's sprint car. Bromme had offered him the *Deck Manufacturing Spl.*, a well-used but decent machine, for the 1951 AAA National Championship season opener at Indy, and Rodger moved to Indianapolis. It had been built and entered by Lou and his son Bruce, who were veterans of West Coast short track racing and did all the work on their cars.

"Lou and Bruce were really the great people. Wonderful people," Rodger recalled. "I helped them finish it up, I painted it. They were working on the car and had a lot to do. They rebuilt it in 1951 and made a lot of changes in the car." He painted the machine red and highlighted it with a black scallop on its nose.

Bruce had been a flight engineer during the war, and now worked full-time at Hughes Aircraft. Rodger counted on him for advice as he took to the Speedway for the first time. Drivers were more open with each other then than they are today, and most weren't afraid to help a rookie. So, Rodger also turned

Roger Ward
Indianapolis Motor Speedway
1951

to gruff Mauri Rose, who explained that driving a front-wheel-drive car took a different technique than he was used to. Even so, Rose said, "The thing you have to understand is that the exit speed in the turn is all that counts." Same as in any car.

The three-time winner explained how to look at the tach at a certain part of the track exiting turn two, and note the engine's rpm. If he could increase his rpm at that point, his lap speed would go up. This could be done by varying the car's line entering the corner, and getting back onto the gas earlier in the corner. Rose said it mattered little how fast he went into the turn; it was how much speed he could carry out of the turn that would get Rodger down the straightaway quicker.

The guidance helped, and Rodger was among the first rookies to pass the new 40-lap test (segments at 100, 110, 115, and 120 miles per hour; 10 laps each) that the AAA had instituted for new drivers. Gaining confidence, he qualified on the second Sunday of the three qualifying weekends (as 1951 was the only year in which qualifying rounds were scheduled over three weekends) with a respectable speed: 134.867 miles per hour and seventh fastest overall. One story has veteran starter Seth Klein, who traditionally gave each rookie driver a short briefing on procedure before their qualifying run, approaching Ward as he was ready to be pushed away. But Ward interrupted with,

Above: Rodger qualified 25th for the 1951 Indianapolis 500. It was his second race in the AAA National Championship series. He dropped out with a broken oil line after 85 miles. *IMS Photos*

Below: Rodger being interviewed on the Speedway's public address system after qualifying. The Offy-powered Bromme was built in California by Lou Bromme and his son, Bruce. Lou is leaning over the back of the cockpit in the white T-shirt and light hat, Bruce is in the white T-shirt and dark hat on the side. The car was raced for more than a decade, competing in 89 championship events. Fitted with a Chevy engine, its last attempt was at Sacramento in 1963, with Bobby Hogle at the wheel. But the car was clearly outdated and not fast enough to qualify for the starting field. *IMS Photo*

"I'll take it the second time around," referring to the starter's green flag. Klein remarked to another official, "That's one fellow I won't worry about in this race."

Despite lining up 25th on the grid—inside the ninth row, since he hadn't qualified on the first weekend—Rodger threw caution to the wind. In the first 2 1/2 miles, he overtook 22 cars and was third at the end of the first lap. But his good fortune didn't last long.

"The motor in that car was absolutely unbelievable. Oh God, down the straightaways you could pass anybody. We broke a rear crossmember and the brake lining. I used to lift at the starting line—maybe a little further down. I was about to pass Joey James. I went right on by, then hit the brakes and didn't have any. You talk about a thrilling moment! I thought I probably could run without brakes for a little while.

"At that time everyone felt that if you were going to go fast here, you don't use the brakes. You don't take your foot off the gas to use the brake. Your left foot is resting on the brake at all times. That was the philosophy. Then I had a couple of other rather interesting experiences. I thought maybe we could fix it.

Methanol Mel Meets Rodger

Midget racing was as competitive and popular in other areas of the country as it was in southern California. One of those hot beds of racing was the Pacific Northwest. In a series of e-mails posted to Yahoo's Racing History group (http://racinghistory.org), midget veteran Mel "Methanol Mel" Anthony recalled when Rodger and several of the other California hot shoes traveled to Seattle for a week of racing, concluding with the Del Fanning Benefit on September 17, 1950. Methanol Mel was at the wheel of the Kurtis that Homer Norman had purchased from Vic Edelbrock. The following is compiled from those e-mails:

"In 1950, at the Sea-Tac Speedway south of Seattle, we had some very fast competition: Shorty Templeman, Don Olds, Paul Pold, Jack Turner, Stan Muir, Wade Althuser, and from Oregon: Len Sutton, Bob Gregg, Louie Sherman, Gordy Youngstrom, Gordy Livingston, and many more from both groups. Lee Madsen, the promoter, invited a group of name cars from California. Allen Heath brought up two cars owned by Lysle Greenman. George Amick drove one, Allen the other. Now if that wasn't tough enough for us, Rodger Ward and Billy Cantrell also came to race. And race we did! Halfway through the show, my good friend Heath and I tangled, as he in the Offy and me in one of the two Fords was a bad fit. He nearly parked in the turns, and I would come in a ton and accidentally punched him out. Heath was then done for the night, except to jump out of the Offy, run to a push truck, and proceed to go after me. I count my blessings he was restrained! Now I began to worry, as Ward and Cantrell were on my rear bumper. I thought it was payback time, but both drivers finally went by cleanly, and after the race I asked Rodger if he saw what took place. Rodger replied that there was no way he would try to take anyone out.

"A week later at our season ending race, [at the Del Fanning benefit] we had a three-car tangle on the front stretch, I got upside down in the [former] No. 27 Edelbrock V8-60. I don't remember anything except getting airborne, then sliding the whole front stretch upside down. As I was lying under the steaming V8-60, Rodger must have been close, jumped from his car, and was the first to me and stopped the overzealous guys from flipping the car off me. He had the presence of mind to realize I could have been injured worse, by not being careful!

"Anyway Jack Turner told me later Ward was mad enough to fight after the race, as his grille got punched out and the nose was caved in. He was especially upset since we were all running for free. I didn't do it, as I was the victim of some bad driving alongside of Jack Turner and I, and I went over the front wheel of Ray Mann's car after someone punched him into me.

"I do remember Shorty won the midget main after the crash, as my wife Barbara gave the trophy before heading to the hospital to check on me! All proceeds went to the late Del Fanning benefit that day."

—Mel Anthony

Rodger had better luck on the dirt at Milwaukee. He qualified third and brought the car home fifth, right behind Paul Russo. *Bob Sheldon photo, Gene Crucean Collection.*

We couldn't," Rodger said. The oil line broke loose after just 34 circuits and he was sidelined. He was awarded 27th position, collecting $2,472 for his efforts, while Lee Wallard scored the victory.

Indy had been on a Wednesday. Ten days later, the national championship reconvened at Milwaukee's 1-mile oval. Bruce asked Rodger to drive again, and he made the most of it. The Bromme chassis worked better on the dirt, and Rodger qualified third fastest. He started the race right behind Jack McGrath, who had earned the pole in Jack Hinkle's Kurtis 4000. He stayed with McGrath and came out of the turn running second. But, as they slowed to enter turn three, McGrath's rear end slipped wide and, with the heavy tank of fuel, it got away from him. He spun to the outside of the track and Rodger dodged past.

In only his third national championship race, Rodger was in the lead. It lasted another 20 laps before Cecil Green in the yellow-and-white, John Zink-sponsored Kurtis passed him. Eventually, Tony Bettenhausen charged to the front, passing Green and taking the win. Tony was wheeling Murrell Belanger's Indy-winning No. 99, after Wallard was burned severely in a sprint car race at Reading, Pennsylvania, just days after Indy.

As the track's surface continued to dry, Rodger fell back and was fifth at the finish.

Rodger then made his first appearance at Langhorne's difficult circular track and qualified the Bromme machine eighth. But he dropped out after 59 laps and earned 18th spot. His luck got worse on the South Carolina pavement at Darlington, where he couldn't find enough speed to make the 4th of July starting field. He was given a second shot in the Hancock Dome Bardazon-Offy, but wrecked while qualifying. In the race, he relieved Cliff Griffith in the Morris Kurtis, putting in 40 laps during the heat of the day. Griffith then brought the car home 11th.

On July 29, he qualified the Bromme third and finished ninth in a non-points race at Pennsylvania's Williams Grove Speedway. Veteran Walt Brown lost his life there when his car rolled over during a practice lap wreck. When Cecil Green and Bill Mackey were killed qualifying at Winchester on the same afternoon, it became known as Black Sunday. Troy Ruttman earned his second national championship victory at Williams Grove and Duane Carter won at Winchester.

Even though he had been performing reasonably well for a rookie on the top circuit in the country, Rodger quickly

Rodger qualified the tan-and-cream-painted Federal Engineering Kurtis 4000 for his second 500 in 1952. After starting 22nd, he was credited with 23rd finishing position. *Armin Krueger.*

learned a tough lesson. He failed to qualify for the next race at the Springfield, Illinois, Fairgrounds and, when Milwaukee came around the second time, he had been replaced by Mike Nazaruk, who was looking for a ride even though he finished second at Indy.

Rodger missed several races before landing in the *Karl Hall Spl.* for the 100-miler at Denver, a new venue on the circuit. The Harry Stevens-built car wasn't highly regarded, as it had failed to make Indy three years in a row before Bill Mackey finally qualified it as the 33rd and slowest starter just five months earlier. Ward qualified 18th and finished four laps off the pace in eighth. He qualified the car in the top 10 for the season's final three races, but dropped out early with mechanical problems twice and finished 10th when he returned to Phoenix.

1952

Beginning with Altoona's board track in 1927, Russ Snowberger raced in 44 championship events. In 1931, he had qualified on the pole at Indy driving a car he built himself that was powered by a Studebaker engine. Although he continued to compete in the Pikes Peak Hill Climb for several more years, Snowberger finished his Indy driving career behind the wheel of the Federal Engineering supercharged Maserati in the 1947 500. He stayed on to run the two-car Federal Engineering team and hired Rodger to drive the team's tan-and-white Kurtis FF4000 for 1952.

At Indy, Rodger qualified in the eighth row, but was in the pits after the first 50 miles with a broken brake line and a leaking oil plug. He ultimately lasted 130 laps before retiring when his mount lost oil pressure. He was scored in 23rd. Significantly, the race focused on a battle between two of Ward's toughest competitors in the midgets. Bill Vukovich looked to have the race securely put away when, with slightly more than eight laps remaining, a steering failure put him into the wall, giving Troy Ruttman the victory.

The rest of the year was as frustrating for Rodger as Indy had been. The high point was at Milwaukee in August, when he turned 30 laps in front of the field after the leaders pitted under yellow just before mid-race. With fresh tires, Chuck Stevenson passed Rodger on lap 106 and led the rest of the way to earn his first championship victory, while a lap behind him Ward faded to seventh. Stevenson would go on to edge Ruttman for the national title in the last race of the year.

At the race in Denver a month later, Rodger moved to the second *John Zink Spl.* entered by M. A. Walker and teamed with Jimmy Reece. Mike Nazaruk hadn't been able to get the car into the field at Indy earlier in the year. With a different driver at each subsequent race, it had only made the field once, with Danny Oakes aboard at Raleigh, North Carolina. Rodger wasn't able to cure the car's ills. He was back in Dobry's Kurtis for the next race at San Jose, but finished last when the gearbox failed after eight laps. He closed the season on an up-note when he gave the Zink-sponsored car its best run of the year, finishing ninth at Phoenix.

1953

Rodger's racing career turned in a positive direction in 1953. He picked up a ride in the new Kurtis of the M. A. Walker team and rejoined chief mechanic Ernie Casale. While the M. A. Walker Electric Company was actually owned by both Marcus and Alfred Walker, Alfred focused on managing the busy business of installing electric wiring in Oklahoma City tract housing, while older brother Marcus ran the racing team. They had gotten their feet wet with a successful postwar midget operation that fielded cars for Ruttman, Reece, Cecil Green, Buzz Barton, and Jud Larson. Jack Zink's first Indy involvement had been as a sponsor for the Walker machines the year before.

In an uneventful month, Rodger qualified the blue-and-white No. 92 car for the 10th starting position at Indy. It was the first time he qualified for the front half of the field, and a lot of the credit was due to Casale's preparation. He had come close to driving Casale's midget several years before and was pleased they were now together on the national circuit.

The 1953 Memorial Day race is widely remembered as one of the most brutal in history. The temperature exceeded 90 degrees Fahrenheit early in the day, and on the track it was measured in excess of 130 degrees. However, these details do little to convey the challenges that the drivers faced. In *Floyd Clymer's Indianapolis 500 Mile 1953 Race Yearbook*, a writer succinctly described the afternoon, his typewritten words fresh from the ordeal (Clymer 1946–1969).

"The story of the race was the heat. When a driver dies from its effects and such experienced competitors as Sam Hanks and Johnnie Parsons are in a state of collapse as they surrender their cars, the full extent of the sun's ruthlessness must be realized. There have been hotter days on which the 500-mile race has been run, but none more humid and stifling."

When Michigan's Carl Scarborough pitted on lap 70, the fuel tank overflowed and a fire erupted, which was quickly put out with carbon dioxide. The veteran of the outlaw sprint car tracks was lifted from his car and taken to the trackside hospital with a body temperature nearing 104 degrees. With three emergency room physicians treating him, even an open-heart massage was unable to revive the silver-haired driver, who was officially listed as 38 years old.

Stock Car Champion in '51

During the summer of 1951, Rodger competed in the AAA's second year of sanctioning stock cars, at the wheel of an Oldmobile 88 sponsored by John Quaden, a local Olds dealer. The series consisted of just three races, all on Milwaukee's dirt mile. Rodger won the first race, a 150-mile event on July 15 that paid $1,625 to win. After running 12th in the first event, 28-year-old Norm Nelson, Rodger's teammate from nearby Racine, Wisconsin, was the first to the checkers in the next race, a 100-miler on August 23. Nelson was disqualified, though, following a post-race inspection of the top three cars conducted at Quaden's garage. Nelson had been using a 4.10 gear instead of the specified 3.90 ratio. Ward who finished second, was declared the winner. Rodger didn't run the third race held the next day, which was also a 100-mile event, but it didn't matter as he had earned the AAA championship.

Rodger's Way

Crew chief Russ Snowberger leans in to find out what's going on. Rodger was sidelined after 120 laps when the car lost oil pressure. *IMS Photos*

Driver Andy Linden's experience was more common. Linden hit the wall in his own car during the early laps of the race, and suffered second-degree burns on his right arm, chest pains, and a general shaking up. Still, he relieved Chuck Stevenson on lap 96, becoming the third driver of the Zink car. But after just 11 circuits, that car retired because of overheating. Nine laps after bringing the Zink car in, Linden was grabbed to jump in Rodger's machine. He put in 70 miles in the cockpit of the Walker Kurtis before coming in for relief and being taken back to the hospital for treatment of heat exhaustion.

In the race Rodger ran well, staying in the top 10 until the 30-lap mark and then running 11th before making his first pit stop just before the 50-lap mark. In the heat of the day, he brought the car back to ninth spot before running into difficulty. After a tire change, he returned for one adjustment, then another, and finally was relieved by Linden. The four pit stops in just 22 laps dropped the car in the running order.

Rodger was taken to the trackside hospital for a treatment of cold iced sheets to reduce his body temperature. Duke Dinsmore added nine more laps after relieving Linden, then Rodger returned to his pit, ready to complete the final 46 laps of the race. But the car quit running on lap 177 and rolled to a stop on the backstretch grass, yet another victim of the heat.

At the traditional victory banquet the next night, Rodger collected $2,916.97 for 16th position.

Having grown up in Fresno's intensely hot climate, Vukovich was untouchable. He led all but five laps, giving it up only when he made his first pit stop. His dominance was such that he lapped the field before the halfway point and that his two subsequent stops could be made without giving up the point. Vuky finished more than 3 1/2 minutes ahead of runner-up Art Cross.

Ward liked Milwaukee's dirt oval, which hosted the year's second race. Surprising many, he was second quickest in qualifying and started on the front row. Pole-sitter Manny Ayulo beat Rodger into the first turn, but Rodger claimed the lead just four laps later. Jack McGrath took up the chase and, when the Offy in Rodger's car let go on lap 15, McGrath was in front the rest of the day.

The torrid heat experienced at Indy continued throughout the Midwest. Springfield, the third championship race of the season, was another brutal scorcher. *Speed Age*'s Bob Russo speculated that it could have been the first time in history a promoter would have welcomed rain. Even though promoter J.

The day after the Memorial Day 500-miler, Troy Ruttman poses in front of the Pagoda in the winning Agajanian Kuzma. Proud car owner J. C. Agajanian would visit Victory Lane a decade later with Parnelli Jones. Standing behind Ruttman is chief mechanic Clay Smith. *Author Collection.*

Rodger was assigned the ride in M. A. Walker's new Kurtis for Indy in 1953. He started 10th and finished 16th after dropping out on the 178th lap. *Author Collection.*

C. Agajanian had the Illinois State Fairground track watered all week, the drivers faced a parched clay surface.

In spite of the dust that was already forming, Ward qualified third fastest. Don Freeland put Bob Estes' A. J. Watson-built car on the pole with McGrath outside. Rodger was flanked by Stevenson in Agajanian's No. 97 Kuzma, with Jimmy Reece and Sam Hanks lined up in the third row.

Bob Russo related Clay Smith's banter surrounding Walt Faulkner's last-row Hart Fullerton ride, which had been driven by Marshall Teague at Indy. Where Teague's name had been removed, only the word "driver" remained. "I finally figured it out, Walt," said Smith. "They've got instructions lettered on your machine. You sit where it says 'driver'. Over here they'll print 'engine', back here, 'gas', and over there, 'oil'. How can you miss?" chided Smith.

Surrounded by a huge cloud of red dust as the 100-mile race started, McGrath surged ahead as Rodger settled in behind Freeland, Stevenson, and Hanks. McGrath had already lapped

Spider Webb, the slowest qualifier, when Reece spun to bring out the caution on lap five. Reece told officials he had lost control when he was unable to see going into the turn.

McGrath was overtaken by Freeland on lap 17, but Stevenson quickly steamed past both of them and surged into the lead, while Hanks and Ward closed the gap to the leaders. Hanks passed McGrath on lap 32 and, within two more laps, Ward had gotten around both McGrath and Hanks for third. Next, he caught Freeland and claimed second, and then took off after Stevenson. On the 43rd lap, he closed on the leader's tail and made the pass as they came off turn two.

With the track becoming more arid as the race progressed, the churning dust thrown up by the cars was just one of the challenges the drivers faced. They skated through the turns as if on ice. Yet, Ward built a half-lap lead while the Flying Dutchman, Tommy Hinnershitz, charged past Freeland for third. On the 55th circuit, Ward continued to lengthen his lead and put McGrath a full lap down.

Stevenson made a 35-second pit stop when he threw the tread from his right rear tire and slipped back to seventh. Jerry Hoyt had the Zink Kurtis 400 up to fourth on lap 77 when a collapsed wheel turned the car into the inside fence, then back

Left: Ernie Casale, crew chief for M. A. Walker's No. 92, ran a number of midgets in URA and AAA in the late 1940s. In 1948, he had obtained a third car and offered Rodger the chance to drive it when he wasn't already busy in other cars. Rodger helped Casale by painting the midget in Casale's traditional colors, blue and white. The night before Rodger's first race in Casale's midget, he was injured at Balboa Stadium in a wreck with Jimmy Bryan. When he was ready to race again, the car was no longer available. *Armin Krueger*

Below: Car owner Marcus Walker (back to camera) congratulates Rodger after his qualifying run. It was Walker's first year at Indy with his own car. Smiling, in the dark shirt behind the Firestone technician at the right rear tire, is one of the leaders of the legendary "Chicago Gang" of midget racers, "Cowboy" O'Rourke. Hatless and leaning toward the cockpit on the right, next to the fellow in the foreground with the white hat, is young John Cooper, who was a stooge on the team. Cooper later became one of the top executives in racing, serving as president of both Indianapolis Motor Speedway and Daytona International Speedway. *IMS Photo*

across the track and through the outside fence. It continued down a hill outside the track and ended against a telephone pole. Hoyt was taken to a local hospital with a possible broken collarbone. Hinnershitz pitted the Dr. Sabourin car under the yellow. Although it was leaking fuel, Frankie DelRoy dumped enough in for the final 20 miles.

With 10 laps to go, the scoring became confused as Ward put Freeland a lap down, leaving Hanks the only car still on the same lap. Russo reported, "Although Ward still led, someone got mixed up and Hanks received the white flag first. Hanks appeared amazed as [Bill] Vandewater threw him the checker ahead of Ward."

Both drivers pulled into victory lane as the confusion grew. Aggie, natty in a cream suit and polka-dot shirt in spite the heat, offered joint custody of the trophy while scorers went back to work. "I had passed Hanks about halfway and he never passed me after that," Rodger said, confidently.

When they discovered that one of the scorers had failed to credit Ward with a lap, the first two positions were reversed, although the rest were not changed. In his 26th national

Rodger, at the right of the photo, races behind Jack McGrath and Duane Carter, driving relief for Sam Hanks. The 1953 race was the hottest 500 on record, with temperatures in the high 90s. This necessitated an unusual number of relief drivers. Both Andy Linden and Duke Dinsmore relieved Ward during the middle stages of the race. McGrath finished fifth without relief, and Hanks' car was third after Carter took over on lap 152. *IMS Photo*

championship race attempt, this was the first national championship win of Rodger's career. Previously, his best finish had been a fifth he took in his third start, which had also been his only top-five result.

While there were a number of bizarre events during racing's first half-century, the next championship race, at Detroit, ranks among any of them. Despite extraordinary efforts, promoter Sam Nunis' track disintegrated in the early laps of the race. The horse-racing surface became a mess of ruts and potholes that shook the cars from their rigid frames to the driver's teeth. Jack McGrath and Paul Russo both withdrew in less than 50 laps because of the roughness, and several cars were sidelined with broken shocks and shock mounts.

Ward started third, behind Duane Carter and newcomer Johnny Fedricks, but Johnnie Parsons raced past them on the backstretch into the lead. Bounding over the deepening holes, Rodger worked on Parsons until he got past on lap 31. With the track getting worse, AAA officials red-flagged the race after 50 laps, one short of an official event.

While the track was watered, crews set about repairing damaged cars in hopes they'd be able to restart the race. In an interview with Carol Sims, Rodger explained that in an agreement with Nunis and AAA, the drivers would continue the race, but no one was to pass and the purse would be paid based on their positions on lap 51.

Once restarted, Rodger continued to run out front, but second place Allan Heath kept trying to get past, and Rodger had to drive harder than he wanted. Finally, on lap 56 his wheel broke, putting him into the wall. With Heath now in the lead, Ernie McCoy flipped when one of his wheels broke. While he was being removed to the hospital, officials again red flagged the race. This time they decided that since cars had been worked on during the first red flag period, clearly against the regulations, the race would be scored complete on lap 51 and Rodger was a championship winner for the second time in his career.

Another good run followed, this time in the non-points race at Williams Grove. Rodger won the last-chance race to earn his starting spot in the main event. In the 50-lap race, he charged from 13th to finish third, trailing Jimmy Davies and Parsons. Then at Springfield, Rodger charged from ninth to third in the first 11 laps, but a broken connecting rod ended that run after just 33 miles.

Through the second half of the 1953 season, Rodger's results were like a roller coaster. After battling Ayulo and Stevenson for second, engine failure sidelined him at Springfield. Starting 10th on the Milwaukee dirt, Rodger scrapped his way into a wheel-to-wheel dice with Paul Russo for second. "But the pace was too much for tires," *Speed Age* reported, "and Ward was forced to give up the fight while he took on new right shoes." He bounced back to finish sixth, the last car on the lead lap.

Above: Along the backstretch at Indy in 1953 and racing with Duane Carter, who has relieved Sam Hanks in the Bardahl Kurtis. Carter later became USAC's first Director of Competition. Rodger has just come out of the pits after retaking the wheel from Duke Dinsmore. *Armin Krueger*

Left: Don Freeland (38) working the outside while Rodger tries to make something happen on the bottom late in the race at Milwaukee in August 1953. Freeland held off Ward and they finished fifth and sixth. *Armin Krueger.*

As the season approached the final races, Bob Russo of *Speed Age* reported Rodger as one of the logical contenders for the national championship. Russo declared, "Rodger Ward was the sixth prospect, riding in eighth place with 462 points and winning a reputation." He added, "Ward, who won two races this year, was 598 points away from McGrath's lead but his reputation as a hard-charging chauffeur made him a contender for the title."

But a late qualifying number hurt his effort at DuQuoin, Illinois, and his qualifying time wasn't fast enough to make the race. Syracuse looked like it could be Rodger's day, as he qualified seventh. Then on the first lap, he saw Bryan—who was just

to his right—turn sideways in turn three. Just behind him, Stevenson hit Bryan's front wheel and somersaulted over the outside wall, seriously injuring several spectators. After 10 caution circuits, the race was stopped.

When racing resumed, Ward set off after Bob Sweikert, the race leader. After moving to second, a caution flag allowed him to restart on the tail of Sweikert's Dean Van Lines Kuzma. He pressured Sweikert for the next 20 laps, but on lap 48 his helmet took a direct hit from a large mud clod thrown up by another car. Stunned, Rodger slowed and made it to the pits, where, with the memory of Indy still fresh, his crew began pouring water on him and wiping him with wet towels. They quickly helped Rodger out of the car and Bob Scott took over. A four-car wreck further delayed the first championship trail victory for the new team of Sweikert, Al Dean, and mechanic Clint Brawner. Scott finished seventh in the Walker machine, the last car still running and several laps behind.

An eighth place finish in the return of the championship cars to the Indiana State Fairgrounds after a six-year absence would be Rodger's last points finish of the year. At Sacramento,

Sam Hanks' third place run earned the national title when McGrath suffered a broken throttle cable. Rodger then dropped out of the final race when his car's suspension broke on the rough Phoenix clay.

1954

Virtually every veteran racing driver has been involved in an incident where another driver was seriously injured or even killed. Like a complex chemical equation, there are multiple factors and outcomes to every racing incident. By its basic nature, open wheel midgets and sprint car racing is extremely close business. The machines are a foot or two apart and, when you are racing through a corner or on a straightaway, there are times you can look straight into another driver's eyes.

Despite this closeness, racing demands a high level of competitiveness. Quite simply, if you aren't trying your hardest, if you aren't holding your breath and giving 110 percent, other drivers will recognize it like bad body odor. Then you are a sitting duck, an easy target. They will attack your vulnerability every time you are on the track, treating you like a mark from

out of town. The simple word is respect. It isn't the product of good public relations. You either earn it from the cockpit of your race car, or you don't.

A racing driver's response to a bad accident in which he may have had a role reflects that individual's character. At one extreme, countless racers with tons of potential have disappeared from the competitive landscape when they decided that they weren't willing to accept the painful things that happen in this business. On the other extreme, a few people will have a cavalier "it didn't hurt me, too bad for them" attitude. Those who become successful are able to develop a middle ground. They somehow accept that what happened is in the past and know they have to move beyond it in order to continue.

This is all part of the driver's education. No one knows how or when to do these things when he first climbs behind the wheel of a racing machine. Drivers learn by watching others execute a smooth slide job. They learn when a veteran dives under them while racing in a turn and they had no idea they were even close behind. And they learn by trying the same maneuvers themselves.

By 1954, only two drivers had driven in the Indy 500 prior to World War II: Sam Hanks and Paul Russo. Illustrating the turnover in racing's ranks, in the three years in which Ward had driven, 26 rookies started their first Indy event. The 1954 Memorial Day classic would add six more to the competitive ranks of the country's biggest motorsports event. And although the technology of computers and digital electronics was still several years in the future, for the first time at Indy, four cars carried experimental electronic transponders that reported each time they crossed the finish line during the race. Most in racing were suspicious of the ability to keep an accurate track of every car without employing a dozen pencils and scoring pads.

Rodger began the season at the wheel of Dr. Raymond Sabourin's white-and-blue No. 12 dirt car built by Johnny Pawl. Fortunately, he again had Ernie Casale as the mechanic. Sabourin was a prominent New York chiropractor and one of the founders of the popular Auto Racing Fraternity Foundation. Rodger qualified well, just over 139 miles per hour, for 16th starting spot.

Nitromethane had hit the Speedway big time and had a significant impact. It was credited for the huge jump in qualifying

Champion Spark Plugs' Earl Twining congratulates Rodger after qualifying at Indy. Both have their cigars lit. *Armin Krueger*

speeds. Indeed, the slowest car in the race—rookie Frank Armi at 137.6—would have started between Vuky and Agabashian in the front row the year before. At the same time, the explosive "pop" was blamed for the number of camshaft failures experienced before qualifying.

However, nitro was definitely not at fault for Bill Vukovich's engine problems. Not only did Howard Keck's Fuel Injection team find itself trying to figure out a rash of piston problems and cracked blocks, but Vuky also was having difficulty finding the speed he wanted. With factory help from Perfect Circle, Frank Travers and Jim Coons found a fix for the motor after the first qualifying weekend but, as the final qualifying sessions approached, stubbornly refused to try a nitro injection. That left the task of finding speed to Vukovich, and he put the car solidly in the field, but would start from the seventh row, just behind Ward.

Once the race started, Vukovich put himself on a pace that advanced him steadily through the field. Although McGrath led from the pole, Vukovich passed him for the lead just before the

halfway mark. In the end, no one was able to keep pace with Vukovich, who was able to nurse well-worn tires in the closing laps and still put second-place Jimmy Bryan, hobbled by a broken front shock and spring, a lap behind at the checkers. The victory set a record average speed of 130.840 miles per hour for the 500 miles and made him the third back-to-back winner in the race's history.

Rodger fell well back early but climbed as high as 13th by lap 20. Eddie Johnson relieved him on lap 92, putting in 67 laps before Rodger climbed back in. But a dozen circuits later, the Sabourin car was out when it stalled on the backstretch and was scored 22nd.

Demonstrating how different the 500 miles at Indy were for the first two finishers, Bryan skipped the Milwaukee race just a week later to give his bruises and burns additional time to heal, and Al Dean invited Vukovich to be the replacement driver. Milwaukee's mile oval had been paved during the off-season and became one of the few paved tracks on the tour. Vuky put Dean's Kuzma dirt car on the pole and led the first nine laps, but retired when the steering failed. After starting 15th, Ward finished an uneventful 10th.

Langhorne, Pennsylvania's mile dirt oval was a track Rodger never liked. But it was back on the schedule and, with the Sabourin team skipping the trip, he secured a drive in a different car. The 3L Racing team put him in the DA Lubricants car, a year-old machine built by Lou Moore that Potsy Goacher had used to take down a row of fence posts along the backstretch in practice at Indy. It wasn't a great performance, though, as Rodger qualified 12th but finished 16th when he wrecked in the fourth turn on lap 34.

Rodger moved to the No. 81 Central Excavating machine for the race at the 1 1/3-mile at Darlington, but came up short of the speed needed to make the field. It was the dirt car that Cleveland's Pete Salemi had purchased new from Floyd Trevis, who had built it with help from Roy Sherman. Vukovich had driven it at Indy in 1951, and it was now prepared and maintained by mechanic Andy Dunlop. Taking the machine to Williams Grove's annual non-points event, Ward won the third heat race and finished fourth in the 50-lap main event.

National champion Sam Hanks took over the Sabourin car for the next two races, and Ward remained in the Central Excavating ride. But by the time the series arrived at DuQuoin for the annual Labor Day weekend Ted Horn Memorial, Hanks had hung his No. 1 on the Belanger car.

Johnnie Parsons (right) working on Rodger early in the Milwaukee 100. At the end of the race, Ward was 10th and Parsons finished 16th.
Armin Krueger

It was a typically hot and humid afternoon as the cars lined up for the 100-lapper at DuQuoin Fairground mile. While Hanks started second, outside of fast qualifier Don Freeland, Rodger was back in the eighth row right on the tail of Chuck Stevenson in the Agajanian car. Freeland led until his magneto quit, giving Hanks the top spot. Stevenson had steadily picked his way through the field and was battling Bryan for second. Although Ward had climbed to a top-five position, his brakes went away and he began to fall back. Choosing to stay on the track to get the best finish he could, Rodger was trying to hold a decent pace and at the same time stay out of the way of faster cars when the unthinkable happened.

DuQuoin Fairgrounds were only a couple hours' drive from Larry Wright's home near Evansville, Indiana. Larry, the young airman who would have dinner with Ward in El Paso in 1959, was in his early teens watching Bryan and Stevenson chasing Hanks as the laps ran down. From his seat in the main grandstand, just across from the pits, he had a clear view of what happened on lap 79.

"Ward was running more or less as a back marker at the time, because he had lost the brakes but he didn't pull the car in," recalled Wright. "He stayed out of the racing groove and if you know DuQuoin, you know it gets to be rather dry and slick in those long races. Coming off of turn four, he let the car drift wide, right into the path of Stevenson."

As Stevenson shot past him coming off turn four, Ward's right front tire caught the left rear of the Agajanian machine. The impact had little effect on Stevenson, but Rodger's car veered sharply to the left. Once the rear end broke loose, he was just a passenger. Still carrying a lot of speed, the car headed toward the inside guardrail, tail first. It was common practice for crewmen to stand along the inside of the track on the wrong side of the guardrail to signal their driver as he went past.

True Grit

While a driver certainly has to have the physical traits that make a person a successful racer—like superlative eye-hand coordination, mental focus, and the right type of body strength and stamina—it also takes great inner courage. Top drivers are willing to go out on a rough or unprepared racetrack and get everything out of their cars. On road courses, they are willing to go into a blind corner or over a rise at racing speed, trusting they are going to come out the other side. And on ovals, they are ready to go wheel-to-wheel with other racers on a slippery surface, on a heavy, rough track, or on one that changes every few feet. The reason is that there is the possibility the other driver may be a little uncomfortable, or has a car that isn't working very well, or makes a mistake, and then bang! you are past and looking ahead to the next car.

A successful racer will purposely position his car to put the other guy in a difficult or risky position and hope the driver will blink and open the door for the pass. Or a driver might attempt to surprise another driver and seize a tactical advantage in a turn when the other driver isn't expecting it. It is at times like these that accidents happen. They are called accidents because no one would cause one on purpose.

"Agajanian's crew, with crew chief Clay Smith, was out there. They were giving a signal to Stevenson as he came along," Wright continued. "Rodger's car spun backwards into that pit. J. C. got over the short fence and cleared the deck real quick. But Clay didn't see it in time to make the move to get out of the way. Rodger's car went backward into the fence at that point and the tail of the car hit Clay where he was standing. He literally got entangled in the rear suspension of the car and it just flailed him to death. Rodger stayed in the car and it came to rest on its side, and he went for a long period of time without being attended to himself. The car didn't flip, it just got onto one side. He was sort of hanging out, dazed."

At least eight others suffered serious injuries. Paul Brooks, a mechanic with the Federal Engineering team and good friend of driver Larry Crockett, was one of them, Wright explained. "He was a fairly heavy man, I'd say he was over 200 pounds. That car caught him in a way that it threw him a good 12 to 15 feet off the ground and a few other people as well. I gather that the tail end of the car, when it was making its swath, got up on the fence and the only reason it didn't go over the fence was because of the rear wheels and the momentum that was being used up."

After two laps under the caution, the race was stopped. Hanks was the winner, but there weren't any victory celebrations. Clay Smith had shared an Indy victory with Ruttman and Agajanian in 1952 and was one of the most popular regulars on the circuit. He had been killed instantly.

Stevenson came to a stop on the front stretch, just a few feet from where Wright was sitting. Wright recalls, "He got out of the car, took off his helmet, gloves, and goggles and went over to the lagoon in the middle of the track and pitched them into the water. He quit from that day. He was just so upset over the accident.

"Really, Rodger was kind of foolish for being out there with no brakes, but that wasn't that uncommon," Wright concluded. "I know that Andy Dunlap was the kind of mechanic who would not have been happy with a driver who pulled in just because he had no brakes. That would have upset him. And those were the days when [Rodger] was attempting to establish himself and I'm sure that he didn't feel for a moment that he was endangering anybody. It was one of those freaky things, just the timing of the whole deal. But it was ugly."

Years later, Rodger admitted that the most difficult time of his life was in 1954 and 1955. He told Carol Sims, "Clay Smith was a man that I greatly admired. I thought he was just the neatest guy there ever was. However inadvertently you're involved in something like that, the fact that you are is a very, very difficult thing" (Wallen 1993).

The damage to Pete Salemi's car was repaired, but Rodger suffered mechanical problems in the next three races. At the Indiana State Fairgrounds Hoosier Hundred, he was up to fifth after starting ninth, when the engine seized on the last lap. As it came to a stop, he jumped out and ran up the track to warn others of his disabled machine.

As the series headed west for the last races of the season, Salemi kept his car at home and Rodger returned to the seat of the M. A. Walker Kurtis. After a rear end failure at Sacramento, he was one of 14 drivers, mostly at the tail end of the qualifying line, who timed too slow to make the field at Phoenix. Then he finally had another good run in Las Vegas

and earned fourth-place money to bring down the curtain on a frustrating season.

His old buddy from the midget-racing days, Jimmy Bryan, added four wins in the last four races to an earlier victory at Langhorne and claimed the national championship for Dean and Brawner. He was the third of Southern California's URA and AAA midget regulars, with Parsons in 1949 and Hanks in 1953, to win the national title.

Rodger was a bachelor and still clearly enjoyed the good life. Yet he said that he was a loner. He had few friends and avoided the cliques that most of the traveling band found themselves in. He enjoyed being a natty dresser, always on the edge of fashion. He was known to regularly stay out late and dated a variety of women in every town he hit. As Rodger admitted, when others found fault with his lifestyle he rebelled, becoming even more obnoxious.

Rodger Ward & Crew
Indianapolis Motor Speedway
=1955=

Rodger drove the *Aristo Blue Spl.* in 1955. The car was co-owned by
Lysle Greenman and Ernie Casale. After starting 30th, Rodger was
involved in the lap 57 accident. The crewmen include Rodger's younger
brother, Ronnie (third from left). *IMS Photo*

Chapter 4

Dark Hours

In 2001, Rodger related the story of Vic Edelbrock visiting Indianapolis during May 1953. "I said, 'You know Vic, you ought to build one of these race cars; we could blow their asses off.' He really gave it some very serious thought. But his health was beginning to go away. We talked about it when I got back to California. He let me know that, because of the problems with his health, he didn't think it would be a project. He said, 'With the amount of attention that I would require to do it well, it probably would stress me a little more than I should be stressed.'

"If he'd have built me a race car for Indianapolis, I'd have won that [race] in the middle-50s. What a guy! He was one of those absolute first-class people," Rodger concluded.

The *Aristo Blue* was sponsored by cowboy movie star Hoot Gibson, who named it after his chinchilla ranch. Gibson visits with Ward along pit lane at Indianapolis. *IMS Photo*

1955

With the new year, Rodger was frustrated with not being selected for any of the new roadsters being prepared. He had been a regular on the trail for four seasons and had proven he could win, but others—such as Bryan, Jim Rathmann, Freeland, Bob Sweikert, Jimmy Daywalt, Art Cross, Pat O'Connor, and rookie Johnny Boyd—were getting the rides with

the teams like Zink and Sumar that were emerging as serious championship contenders.

He reunited with chief mechanic Ernie Casale, who was orchestrating a promising opportunity. Lysle Greenman had purchased the Agajanian car that Troy Ruttman drove to victory at Indy in 1952 and in which Walt Faulkner broke all the Indy records the year before that. With sponsorship from Hollywood cowboy Hoot Gibson, who named it the *Aristo Blue Spl.* after his chinchilla farm, the Kuzma-built dirt machine should have been better than it was. Perhaps it was the result of passing through several hands after Clay Smith had prepared it for Ruttman and Stevenson, but the car proved to be a real handful when at speed. And as Rodger noted, it didn't get any better as the month of May progressed.

In spite of a stellar cast of characters, including Bettenhausen, Bryan, Hanks, Faulkner, Cross, and Pat Flaherty, the focus of the Indianapolis race appeared to be on Vukovich's quest for a third straight win. And it seemed, from the time that the track officially opened, the driver with the best opportunity to stop him would be Jack McGrath. Both had strong hands coming in: McGrath in the Kurtis 500C he drove the year before (courtesy of Jack Hinkle), and Vukovich moving with mechanics Jim Travers and Frank Coons (both were on leave from a delayed streamliner project Howard Kech was pursuing) to drive Lindsey Hopkins' Kurtis 500C, driven in 1954 by Pat O'Connor.

Only Jerry Hoyt and Tony Bettenhausen qualified on pole day, as the others agreed to wait for better weather. The next day, the speedsters left their mark, as McGrath's 142-mile-per-hour average led Fred Agabashian and Vukovich as the only drivers to qualify at over 141 miles per hour. Rodger's 135.049 average was more than 4 miles per hour slower than his official speed the year before, and he started outside the 10th row.

McGrath claimed the lead before the first turn and it didn't take more than a lap before he and Vuky were running first and second. But the anticipated battle was as short-lived as it was intense. As Bob Russo reported in *Speed Age*, "Vukie was nearly to the starting line on the fifth lap when McGrath appeared out of the turn in a cloud of smoke which poured from under the hood of his yellow No. 3."

The first symptoms of mechanical problems were in evidence, yet out of frustration McGrath willed his smoking mount ahead of Vukovich on the backstretch just nine circuits later. Vuky fought back, re-passing McGrath, and opened his biggest lead. But as they sliced through packs of slower cars, McGrath kept pace with the blue Hopkins machine. With the smoke appearing to abate, he retook the lead on lap 25, only to have Vukovich go back in front 5 miles later while cutting the fastest lap of the race. After a caution lap for Agabashian's spin, Vukovich built a 10-second advantage as McGrath became more concerned about making his car last as long as possible. Finally,

The *Aristo Blue* was the Kuzma dirt car that Troy Ruttman drove to victory in the 1952 Indy 500. *Armin Krueger*

Left: Ernie Casale (center) is talking with Rodger after a practice run. Casale and Lysle Greenman joined forces for the first time to field the *Aristo Blue*. Casale's son, Andy, said Greenman had more of a financial stake in the partnership, and Casale managed the team and was the chief mechanic. *Rodger Ward Jr.*

Right: Casale (left) was successful at giving young midget racers a taste of Indianapolis by putting them on his pit crew. He found them to be enthusiastic, skilled, and hard working. Next to Casale is one of those crewmen, California midget regular Edgar Elder. On the right is Don Anderson, a Los Angeles police officer who frequently helped Casale with his midgets and had been involved in a widely reported gunfight early in the year. *IMS Photo*

McGrath headed to the pits and climbed from his car, victimized by a magneto failure.

Already three laps behind, Rodger came off the second turn on the leader's 57th lap. Johnny Boyd saw Rodger's car veer sharply to the right, just ahead of him and Al Keller, and start flipping. Russo wrote, "Moving onto the backstretch, Ward's car broke an axle. The speeding mount went out of control, despite Ward's desperate efforts to correct it, and slammed into the outside guard rail."

One credible study of the circumstances states that evidence points to Ward losing control when hit by a gust of wind, buoyed by the fact that Agabashian had reported wind and a greasy track as causing his spin minutes earlier. Rodger was quoted in the next day's newspaper, stating, "I was coming out of the Southeast Turn, when the wind got me."

Rodger was also cited in other interviews as saying the right front axle broke. In reality, the situation was more complex than that. "The right front spindle wiggled around," he once explained. "I could hardly keep the goddamned thing straight down the straightaway. I was really upset. Finally, over in turn two, I got out a little bit against the wall and spun the car."

In any case, his car turned, hit the fence south of the backstretch footbridge, and began flipping. While Ward's dirt car barrel-rolled along the rail, Keller and Boyd steered to the inside as they exited the second turn. But, when Keller got two wheels on the grass and used his hand brake, his car broke loose. As he tried to collect it, his car turned abruptly into Boyd's machine. Keller slammed Boyd's left front just as Vukovich, who had committed to passing inside of Ward's machine to avoid the debris along the fence, rushed up behind them.

With the track suddenly blocked, Vuky instinctively tried to turn back to the right, but Boyd's machine was shoved directly into his path, the right rear tire serving as a launching mechanism for Vukovich's nose. The blue Kurtis climbed on top of the outside wall and turned toward the parked cars, barely missing the abutment for the footbridge. It is likely Bill suffered a basal skull fracture on the first hard impact and didn't feel the pin-wheeling ride or the fuel fire that erupted as the car stopped.

Ward's machine stopped sliding just as the flipping cars of Boyd and Vukovich tumbled past. Boyd later told a newspaper that after Keller helped roll his car over and he had started yelling at him, Rodger came up and told him to get off the

Just moments after the tragic Vukovich wreck on lap 57. Rodger's car (27) still sits in the middle of the track after hitting the fence and flipping twice. The 39, farther down the track (top photo), is the Sumar Kurtis that rolled three times with Johnny Boyd in the cockpit. On the left, at the edge of the track, an ambulance is heading toward Keller's car, which is surrounded by emergency workers. Closer on the left (bottom photo) is Elisian's car (68); he stopped at the edge of the track to lend assistance. Tire tracks and debris (top photo) show the path Vuky's car took as it narrowly missed the overhead bridge and began somersaulting over the backstretch fence.
Armin Krueger

It has been reported that after being released from the trackside hospital, Rodger was found wandering Gasoline Alley in a daze. Here he has taken a shower and changed his clothes and is talking with Johnny Boyd at the door of his garage stall. Boyd, who was a rookie in the race, has apparently just been released from the infield hospital and is still shirtless and wearing his dirty driving pants. *Rex Dean Collection*

A Bad Decision

The death of Bill Vukovich had a profound impact on Rodger. While he admitted to himself that people said he was doing too much drinking and running around, he knew they were wrong. He had been told that he wouldn't be able to last a full 500 miles, which he hadn't yet. And even though his car's handling suffered from a bad vibration, he had purposely decided to stay on the track until it fell apart. Years later, he told Carol Sims, "I should not have been on the racetrack in that car, but I was. I knew it was bad; actually the front axle broke right at the kingpin which caused the thing to go out of control" (Wallen 1993).

track before he got killed. However, photos show Ward walking with safety officials along the service road toward the ambulance where Boyd was already being attended.

Rodger was examined in the infield hospital and released with just scrapes and bruises, while young, hard-charging Bob Sweikert drove to victory in John Zink's rose-and-white-colored Kurtis. It was the first trip to Indy's victory lane for chief mechanic A. J. Watson, who just days before the race had flown to California to be with his wife and left Sweikert to assemble the winning Offy engine.

It was a somber victory, though. A two-time Indy winner and a midget champion, Vukovich was highly liked and greatly respected throughout the racing community. Concluding his report in *Speed Age*, Russo wrote that at the traditional victory dinner, Sweikert praised his crew, calling each by name. Then "his voice became unsteady and he choked up with tears as he said: 'I'd be more than happy to give up first place if only Billy could be here.'"

Over the next couple of days, Rodger told close friends he was thinking of giving up racing. But at Vuky's funeral in Fresno on Saturday, Bill's brothers Eli and Mike, whom Rodger knew well from their midget days, met with him quietly and persuaded him to continue.

"That damned near ended my racing career," he recalled years later. "I didn't believe that I could be a part of that unfortunate incident. I knew Vukovich well. I had raced against him in midgets for years. When I got busted up at Sacramento, Bill was one of the first people who got to me."

The *Aristo Blue* Kuzma was repaired and towed to Milwaukee. Rodger didn't have the qualifying speed to make the field, but he and his team ran a 20-lap semi for the non-qualifiers. Reportedly, the kingpin broke during the semi and when Rodger refused to drive the car again, he was fired on the spot. Johnny Thomson, who had raced from last to second at Indianapolis, took his first national championship win there.

As the schedule pointed toward Langhorne, Ward returned to the cockpit of Pete Salemi's Central Excavating Trevis. Ironically, it was the same car Vukovich had driven in 1951,

Rodger Ward & Crew
Indianapolis Motor Speedway
=1956=

when he, Rodger, Salemi, and the car were all rookies. Rodger registered a ninth place finish in his reunion with mechanic Andy Dunlop.

In September, Ed Walsh put Rodger in his KK4000 at Syracuse, and Jimmy Reece moved to the Ray Brady car. Reece had earned two top-10 finishes in the car since Indianapolis, but had been too slow to make the DuQuoin field the week before. Rodger took a ninth in his first outing with Walsh and added a sixth at Phoenix to close the season. His career didn't appear headed anywhere in particular, although he felt the late season rides in Ed Walsh's Kurtis had allowed him to once again show that he could finish well when given a chance.

Going for a second consecutive title, Bryan was referred to as "perhaps the most feared competitor on the Championship Trail today," by *Speed Age*'s Bob Russo. He scored wins at Langhorne, Williams Grove, Springfield, DuQuoin, the Indianapolis Fairgrounds, Sacramento, and Phoenix, giving him a dozen wins in just two years. But Sweikert added a victory at Syracuse to his 500 win and claimed the national championship.

The Power of Jo

While auto racing in America was altered forever with the introduction of USAC, Rodger's life was changing nearly as significantly. During the 1955 season, he married a young lady he had dated several years earlier. Josephine "Jo" Walton was a Los Angeles law student and bookkeeper. During World War II, she worked as a civil servant in the Army's G-2 branch, processing troop movements. During this time, she was attacked and savagely beaten, spending three weeks in the hospital with military police guarding the door to her room.

Later, Jo contracted tuberculosis while assigned in Japan and was returned to a sanitarium in Los Angeles. Although few knew it at the time, Rodger visited regularly during her lengthy hospitalization. She had been at the 1955 Indy 500 and they were married three weeks later, during one of the lowest periods of Rodger's career.

A Quaker, Jo demanded a different lifestyle than Rodger was used to. He was 34 years old and in many ways, she pushed him into maturity. He embraced many changes. He had given up smoking while visiting her in the hospital and on New Year's Eve he quit drinking. He was settling down. Such was his transformation that the bio in the 1956 *Floyd Clymer's Indianapolis 500 Mile Race Yearbook*, right after noting his skill at gin rummy and golf, included the statement, "Bent on staying in top physical shape, he does not smoke or drink, and works out regularly during the off season."

As he had during the previous 12 months, Rodger continued to tour with Irish Horan's Hell Drivers when he wasn't racing. Horan, who had gotten his start as the press agent for Tom Mix's Circus, was well known as a public address announcer at the Indianapolis Motor Speedway. For years he operated a traveling thrill show known for shooting a car out of a cannon and later the Jimmy Lynch Death Dodgers. Rodger's specialties were precision driving routines and handling cars with their two right-side wheels high in the air. The newlyweds moved into an apartment complex just off 16th Street in Indianapolis, and Jo frequently went on the road with Rodger.

It had been a difficult year for racers. Larry Crockett and Mike Nazaruk were killed a week apart in sprint car races at Langhorne, even before Indianapolis. Manual Ayulo, another California racer who had competed with Rodger in midgets, lost his life during qualifying at the Brickyard. A highly publicized accident during the running of the 24-hour race at Le Mans resulted in 80 dead. It seemed like the bad news wouldn't stop. As the season neared its end, the AAA announced it was ending its involvement in motorsports. A new organization, the United States Auto Club (USAC), began to take shape. Then in the final championship race under AAA auspices, Jack McGrath was killed when the axle on the Hinkle dirt car broke at Phoenix.

1956

The Indianapolis Motor Speedway was changing. In addition to a new administration building and museum at the corner of 16th and Georgetown, new asphalt had been applied to the majority of the 2½ miles, leaving only a section on the main stretch that was still brick, and lap speeds responded.

Rodger remained with Ed Walsh and mechanic Harry Stevens, who brought Walsh's Kurtis KK500C roadster, named the *Filter Queen Special*. The car missed the race the previous year when, with Paul Russo at the helm, it was called in after three qualifying laps; in the long run it would have been fast enough to make the starting grid. When the Speedway opened for practice, Stevens had his car on the oval first for the eighth straight year and, as had become tradition, Stevens was at the wheel for those opening circuits.

The combination of changes was working, as Rodger qualified at 141.171 miles per hour, good for outside of the fifth row. He was in the top 10 by the 150-mile mark and stayed there for the remainder of the race, as he finally went the distance for the first time. Rodger was scored eighth, six seconds behind "Rookie of the Year" Bob Veith, and with an overall time of 1 second over four hours.

There was one other noteworthy change. Starting from the pole, new track record holder Pat Flaherty drove to victory, the second in a row for car owner John Zink and chief mechanic A. J. Watson. Significantly, this winning machine was the first to come from Watson's shop in Glendale, California.

Flaherty also won at Milwaukee, the championship trail's next race. Rodger didn't have a ride at Milwaukee, then missed qualifying the Holynski Kurtis by one spot at Langhorne. However, when Veith's blistered hands became too painful to

Above: Indianapolis, 1956. Rodger heads out to start his qualifying run. *IMS Photo*

Right: The great Jimmy Bryan with his foot on the tire of his car is relaxing with a racing fan. Bryan came out of Arizona to learn his trade in California's midgets and went on to become one of the toughest racers on the championship tour. *Ken Coles*

continue after leading the first 16 laps at Langhorne, Ward was called to drive relief in the Federal Engineering Kurtis. Rodger brought the car home 10th after losing several laps during the driver change.

Darlington was next, and Rodger drove his first race for Indianapolis businessman Roger Wolcott. Rodger handled the Lesovsky dirt car that had been barrel-rolled by Len Sutton the day before qualifying opened at Indy. (It had been repaired.) Then at Milwaukee with Troy Ruttman driving, it lasted until the clutch failed. Ward started fifth at Darlington but, on a brutally hot day, fell back right at the start and was running 20th after just 15 laps. He gutted it out, though, falling five laps behind until an incident on the 141st lap. According to *Speed Age*, "Dick Rathmann and Ward tangled in the middle of the banked turn. Both cars appeared locked together and slid for a few feet before separating. Both of them slid down into the infield where they came to a safe rest."

Telepathy

In a Saturday Evening Post article by Angelo Angelopolous, Rodger revealed that he could feel Jo's emotions while he was racing. During the 1956 Indy 500, he had felt the tension created by an argument between another driver's wife and mother while Jo was seated in a special section for driver's families. From then on, she sat away from the other wives by herself in another spectator area, and worked to remain calm while Rodger was competing.

Crew chief Herb Porter took the Wolcott No. 62 to Atlanta's Lakewood Park dirt mile, where Rodger qualified on the front row. *Speed Age* described the start: "Blasting past the starting line, Ward inched ahead of Veith. Reaching the first turn, a tricky sort of curve that bends sharply and extends into something of a short straightaway, Ward was ahead by nearly two car lengths and pulling away fast."

Rodger maintained the lead with apparent ease, unchallenged as he skillfully negotiated the tricky layout. Then he slowed on the 63rd lap, a telltale puff of smoke providing evidence of a broken cog in the gear tower, and he was scored 16th.

Although Flaherty maintained a healthy 600-point national championship lead, his season came to a crashing end when he flipped at Springfield in August, and his arm was crushed by the car's roll bar. Rodger earned his first finish for Wolcott, bringing the Lesovsky home sixth after starting 15th.

Porter liked the hard-driving Ward in his machines, and Rodger qualified outside the front row for the Hoosier Hundred, the biggest and best paying of the Fairground mile races. But, in his first national championship start, Jud Larson qualified Zink's car on the pole and jumped into the early lead. It took 72 circuits for Jimmy Bryan to work his way into the lead, as Larson began to fade. O'Connor grabbed second and fended off Rodger's late-race challenge. The finish gave Ward his fourth top-10 finish of the season (fifth when counting the non-points race at Williams Grove), while Bryan's fifth victory clinched the second national crown for the Arizona cowboy.

A fuel pump failure sidelined Ward at Sacramento, then came the season-ending round at Phoenix, which started with a tangle before the first turn. The fifth row, Bryan and Bill Cheesbourg got caught up with sixth row starter Elmer George and Rodger—who qualified on the last row—bringing out a red flag. Later in the race, Ward's season concluded when, as Bob Schilling described it, he "went through the fence and into the oleanders" (Wallen 1993).

There was one additional obvious difference at the end of the 1956 season. For the first time, Rodger Ward finished in the top 10 of the final standings, earning eighth. His 862 points were well behind Bryan's 1,860, but it was a milestone nonetheless. At Indy, he had earned membership into the Champion Spark Plug's 100-mile-per-hour club, joining those drivers who completed the full 500 miles. While the century speed mark was not as significant as it had been in the early years of the organization, running the full race remained a considerable

Opposite top left: Rodger and Herb Porter (right) show off the new Wolcott roadster, built by Luigi Lesovsky. With them in their Gasoline Alley garage is Duncan Renaldo, better known in Hollywood as the "Cisco Kid." With the skin removed, the angle in the chassis at which the supercharged Offy was mounted is quite apparent. *Author Collection*

Top right: Public address announcer Irish Horan interviews Rodger after his qualifying run. In addition to being the voice of various racing tracks throughout the year, Horan operated an auto thrill show that appeared around the country and employed Rodger as one of his stars. *IMS Photo*

Bottom: Rodger appears to be in a good mood before qualifying Roger Wolcott's Fuel Injection Special in 1957. On race day the car only lasted 27 laps before the supercharger failed. *Armin Krueger*

accomplishment. And with Roger Wolcott and Herb Porter, Rodger felt he had finally found a home with a team that had the ability to win every time it unloaded its toolbox.

1957

Renovations to the Speedway provided a new and much safer pit lane, separated from the racetrack by a short cement wall. Behind the pits, the modern steel and glass Tower Terrace replaced the Pagoda for race officials. The upgrades included complimentary grandstands on each side of the tower, running the length of the pits.

The success of Watson's Zink roadsters opened the door to several new schools of thought as teams prepared for the 1957 season. With the reduction in engine size (from 274 ci to 256) for the new season and everyone—with the exception of the two 12-cylinder Novis—running Meyer-Drake Offenhausers, car builders were focusing on relatively new areas to gain a competitive advantage.

First, they began seriously looking at reducing car weight, then tailoring the weight's distribution to help the machines through Indy's left-hand turns while also minimizing tire wear. At the same time, as the nation was making initial steps into the space age, car builders became more conscious of the effect of aerodynamics over the car's body. While some became lower and sleeker, others grew large fins in an effort to break up the air behind the car's fuel tank. The width of the new racers averaged 4 inches trimmer than the older machines.

Veteran mechanic George Salih's idea was to lay the powerplant on its side in a very low and lightweight chassis. *Floyd*

Clymer's Indianapolis 500 Mile Race 1957 Yearbook reported the engine was mounted only 18 degrees from being horizontal, allowing the driveshaft to run down the left side of the chassis while the driver was seated to the right of centerline. The hood of the machine was only 22 inches above the racing surface. With Sandy Belond's sponsorship providing funding to complete the project, Quinn Epperly fabricated the body panels. While Sports Illustrated reported the design produced "the lowest profile, but also some of the meanest handling," veteran driver Sam Hanks called it "the finest car I've ever driven."

In building Wolcott's new machine for Rodger, Herb Porter and Luigi Lesovsky took a contrary approach that really maximized the weight on the left side. Their four-cylinder Meyer-Drake

Offy was set about 20-degrees crossways in the chassis, with the front of the engine near the car's left front corner and the transmission pointing toward the right rear tire. Lesovsky positioned the driver's seat on the left and ran the driveshaft along his right side. This approach required two universal joints, one at the end of the transmission to turn the driveline parallel with the frame, and a second at the rear axle. Additionally, Porter added a supercharger to provide a boost for the 170-ci engine. With the white number eight centered in a black circle, the car quickly became known as the 8-Ball.

Ward's Wolcott Fuel Injection Spl. didn't produce the desired results immediately. His qualifying average of 141.321 came on the second weekend and put him in the eighth row for the start.

Bob Wilke (left) presenting the winner's trophy after the Milwaukee 100. Rodger has just claimed the third victory of his career and first in four years. Car owner Roger Wolcott (right) has a firm grip on the hardware. *Armin Krueger*

Left: The ride with Roger Wolcott's team brought a good dirt car, built by Luigi Lesovsky. Chief mechanic Herb Porter is making adjustments under the hood at Detroit. *Ken Coles*

Opposite top: Rodger battles with Jim Rathmann (26) at Milwaukee in June. Rathmann finished fifth in the Epperly. *Armin Krueger*

Opposite bottom: Ward and Rathmann work past Don Branson in Ray Brady's Kurtis. Branson is signaling that his engine has stalled and he's out of the race on lap 52. *Armin Krueger*

But the new ride lasted only 30 minutes into the race, falling victim to a supercharger bearing failure after 27 laps. The resulting 30th position finish would be the worst of Rodger's Indy career.

Contrary to Ward's bad luck, Hanks took the battle to the fast runners: Russo in the Novi, O'Connor, rookie Eddie Sachs, Ruttman, and Jim Rathmann. After taking the lead for the first time on lap 36, Hanks paced all but 29 of the remaining circuits in Salih's creation. In Victory Lane, he tearfully announced his retirement from competition (with the exception of stock car commitments that he later fulfilled).

After skipping Langhorne, Porter had the supercharger problem solved with help from Stu Hillborn, and Ward qualified sixth at Milwaukee. With a performance that proved Porter's design, Rodger hustled to the front while Johnny Boyd scrapped with Bryan for the lead. Rodger caught and passed Boyd, then took the point from the Dean Van Lines car on the 21st lap.

Bryan's race ended in a tangle with Art Bisch. Jim Rathmann challenged Ward, but fell back when his brakes went south. Johnny Thomson took second away from Boyd at the finish. The race paid $5,222 for the win and Rodger posed for many photos with Jo, her dog, Wolcott, and the first place trophy. In each, Rodger is literally beaming from ear to ear; he knew that he had finally found his way back to victory lane.

In late June, the national championship took a short hiatus, as 15 of the top drivers (Bryan, Ruttman, O'Connor, Parsons, Russo, Linden, Bettenhausen, Sachs, Crawford, Veith, Ward, Jim Rathmann, Weyant, Teague, and Mantz) flew to Monza, Italy, for the Monza 500. Only the first 10 actually had their cars and teams transported across the Atlantic and competed, with Bryan

No Risk, No Reward

During a bull session with Rodger in the Indianapolis Motor Speedway's media center in 2001, author Terry Reed asked Rodger about danger and the risks he took in racing.

"When I came here in 1951, I had a sprint car ride that the Brommes owned," Rodger replied. "I ran a race at Dayton. I thought a guy would have to be a brave son of a bitch to run there. I only drove the car a couple of times. I ran at Winchester one time in a midget. Got quick time, won the trophy dash and the main event. Then I said, 'I can't do this. I'm too goddamned old to run the high banks with you fucking kids.' I drove that midget at DuQuoin on the mile and won. In those days we didn't have tires that were nearly as good.

"I never allowed myself to think about it. I felt that I had a handle on what I was doing. I realized that something might happen to the car that would create a problem. I felt that I drove safely enough to stay out of trouble. I did have a few experiences in a midget. I got upside down one time at San Diego and I broke this shoulder. Jimmy Bryan and I were racing and we got the white flag. I went into turn one and Bryan tried to do a slide act on me. Zappo! I was upside down and I was all busted up, saying, 'Get me out of this sum bitch; I'm going to kill him.' I couldn't even walk. But those things happen. Then Jimmy and I became very close friends.

"I wouldn't say that I had a lot of really close friends. McDowell was one of my extra-special favorite people. Tony Bettenhausen and I were [close friends]. On the dirt he was the absolute champion of all. In 1953 we were racing at Syracuse and I passed him on the outside. When the race was over I came over and said, 'Okay, old man. I did get around you on the outside.'

"He said, 'Yeah, you son of a bitch.'

"His death was unreal. A couple of race drivers were killed in cars that I drove. Jimmy Bryan in my dirt car at Langhorne. We used to live up at Lake Shafer in the summer months and water skied and boated. Jimmy had a pretty good boat. We used two lengths of rope, meaning that a skier was 100 feet behind the boat. When the skier did a turn, he was doing 100 miles per hour. When Sachs was out there, Bryan did a turn and Sachs fell off. Bryan said, 'Oh shit. We've killed him.'

"I had this big old Chris-Craft. We had more fun than the law would allow. I've had so much fun in life that it's hard to describe how lucky I've been. I've still got all my pieces. I consider myself one of the exceptionally lucky people in the world. It's still the greatest sport there is."

collecting the victory, having won two of the three legs and completing more laps than anyone else. The Grand Prix stars boycotted the event, but David Murray's Ecurie Ecosse team fielded three Type D Jaguars, fresh from their Le Mans victory.

When the tour regrouped at Atlanta, where Rodger had come so close to winning the year before, it was one of those days drivers would just like to forget about. Rodger qualified fifth, but after completing his run, he caught the wall and took a tumble. The damage was minor, so quick repairs allowed him to start the race. In the early going, he was able to challenge Bryan for second but then he spun out, hitting the wall on the 21st circuit. Elmer George also spun out of the race avoiding him.

In Dick Wallen's *Fabulous Fifties* (1993), Bob Schilling relates that Ward employed a characteristic form of gamesmanship, sharpened from playing gin rummy in Gasoline Alley, to capture the 100-miler at the Springfield Fairgrounds. Ward had qualified fourth and would start behind the front row of

Atlanta-winner George Amick (on the pole), and Elmer George, Tony Hulman's son-in-law. Ward quietly advised young George that if Amick got away early, he would be hard to catch. Ward suggested that George pinch Amick down on the inside at the start and try to take the lead.

George did what needed to be done, accelerating quickly and diving low into the first turn, his left rear just ahead of Amick's right front, forcing Amick to give way. But Ward hadn't told George about part two, where Rodger wound up the Wolcott dirt car and blasted around the top of the first turn with a clean lane ahead and passed both of them for the lead. Without any cautions, Rodger built a sizeable lead and was unchallenged as he scored his second win of the season. Worth

noting, starting 16th and finishing ninth was another A. J.— this one a young Texan in his first championship race. His last name was Foyt.

Returning to Milwaukee for the 200-mile race in August, Rodger was ready to make it two in a row. Exhibiting the confidence that comes from winning, starting 18th didn't bother him. He charged early and was third before the 40-lap mark. He worked past pole-sitter Pat O'Connor and then took the lead from Jim Rathmann shortly after a restart. For 53 laps, all Rathmann could do was try to keep the 8-Ball in sight. Then Rodger suddenly slowed and turned into the pits as a wing nut had backed off the right front wheel and it became obviously loose. Although he rejoined in fifth, the car quickly began overheating and he parked it, finishing where he had started, in 18th.

Next up was DuQuoin, and Rodger out-qualified all but Jud Larson who was in Zink's Watson-built dirt car. Rodger used the

Rodger continued to race midgets every time he could. He started on the pole of the 100-lap midget race during Fair Week at Milwaukee.
Armin Krueger

outside starting spot to grab the lead as he came off the second turn of the mile-long dirt oval. Like Rathmann at Milwaukee, Larson couldn't stay close enough to fight for the lead, so he settled in behind the Lesovsky-built dirt machine to see how the race played out. He was rewarded as the laps passed the halfway mark when Rodger's pace began to slow. As Larson closed in, he could see that a shock had broken on the Wolcott car. Larson took the lead on the 54th circuit, and 20 laps later Thomson claimed second from Ward, which is how they finished.

While Rodger was enjoying the best season of his career, it was flawed by extremes. After running in the lead pack at Syracuse, he was later the first to drop out when his brakes failed after 41 circuits. Even though he had scored two wins and had a third, he was only 12th in the points. The reason was that the other results were as bad as those were good. After

Right: The first victory of 1958 came in the Milwaukee 200. Rodger leads Jim Rathmann in the *Zink Spl. Armin Krueger photo, Gene Crucean Collection*

Below: Rodger is joined in victory lane by Jo, his wife, and Bob Wilke, who presented the Leader Card Trophy, after winning the Milwaukee 200. *Armin Krueger*

Rodger tells it like it was over the track's public address system while Bob Wilke appears deep in thought. Is this the scene Bob was remembering when he hired Rodger to drive for him the next year? *Armin Krueger*

his 30th place at Indy, he finished 16th twice and 18th twice in races that, with just one exception, started only 18 cars.

At the Indiana State Fairgrounds on the near-northeast side of Indianapolis, Wolcott's dirt car overheated again, and Rodger was scored 13th after qualifying third and challenging for the lead. Again, on the newly paved Trenton, New Jersey, mile Rodger charged from 10th to second and was pressing O'Connor for the win when his brakes let him down. He tried to carry the car to the finish, but retired with ignition troubles with only 30 miles remaining and was registered in 20th place.

Rodger celebrated another milestone when he captured his first pole on the championship circuit at Sacramento. Although Amick outran him to the first turn, Ward applied pressure until taking the lead on the 18th lap. Bryan took second, but didn't have anything for Rodger, who scored his third victory of the year.

At Phoenix, Rodger captured his second consecutive pole for the season's final race. But at the start, when trying to stay with Boyd, he slid across the hard track and up into the marbles. By the time he had everything pointed in the right direction, Rodger had fallen back six positions. Bryan scored a memorable victory to sew up his third national championship in four years. Forced out to the wall while trying to lap Jim Rathmann on the 96th circuit, Bryan exited the racing track through a hole in the wooden fencing and rejoined just as quickly through another hole. The only car to pass him during this excursion was Pat O'Connor and it took Bryan just three laps to reclaim the lead.

For the Wolcott team, the season ended somewhat predictably, suffering a gear failure with less than 20 miles to go. While Rodger's three victories topped the national championship series, eight DNFs kept him one spot short of the top 10 in the final USAC standings.

Left: After Indy in 1958, Ray Nichels recruited Rodger to handle tire testing chores for Firestone. Here Rodger, in the special Firestone test car, gets assistance from Don Freeland and Len Sutton. *IMS Photo*

Right: Johnnie Parsons was a midget champion and the 1950 Indianapolis 500 winner. *Ken Coles*

1958

The season opened not at Indianapolis, as it had for most of the past decade, but at Trenton in April. Although Rodger started third, the engine seized just 30 laps into the event and Ward, Porter, and Wolcott began looking toward Indianapolis. Oregon's Len Sutton out-dueled Tony Bettenhausen in the Central Excavating colors to take Pete Salemi and crew chief Andy Dunlop to victory lane.

During practice before Indy qualifying, Rodger had spun the 8-*Ball* into the wall, which was a rare occurrence. But Porter had the car back together in time to qualify for the 11th starting spot. At the start, he was able to avoid any damage during the turn three melee on the first lap. Running in the top 10, Rodger was as high as fourth when the leaders began to make pit stops just before the 50-lap mark. When Rodger made his pit stop, the engine stalled and it took Herb extra time to get it restarted. He was pit-side for a total of 54 seconds. Then, while still running in the top 10, the engine quit as he drove off the second turn on his 94th lap and the car rolled to a stop in the infield.

This time it wasn't related to the Offy or its supercharger. No, this time the fuel pump had failed. He was scored in 20th place.

Once the race restarted, fans were treated to a trophy dash as Bryan, Sachs, Bettenhausen, and Boyd traded the top four positions. Then a decade after they had battled on the dirt bullrings of California, Rodger saw Jimmy Bryan's effort pay off at Indy. Bryan saluted the fans with his trademark both-hands-in-the-air-and-steering-with-his-knees move as he took the checkered flag in the same George Salih-built lay-down machine that Sam Hanks had won with the year before.

Sumar chief mechanic Ray Nichels headed the Firestone racing division's tire testing program and was on the verge of beginning test runs using a new Kurtis-Kraft powered by a custom-built, 485-horsepower Pontiac powerplant. O'Connor had been Nichel's driver and with him gone, Ray hired Rodger to take over the driving duties. Although tedious, Rodger worked hard with Nichels, Firestone's Bill McCrary, and engineer Steve Petrasek and forged a relationship that would pay dividends some years later.

'58 Indy tragedy

The 1958 Indianapolis 500 will always be remembered for what happened during the first 60 seconds of the race. A duel of speed had preceded the race, as drivers pushed each other for the top speed during practice each day, then Dick Rathmann narrowly edged Ed Elisian for the pole position during qualifying.

On race day, Rathmann led the front row away from the starting line ahead of the pace car and then spent frantic moments trying to get back into place just before the green flag. Although Rathmann jumped ahead of the pack before the first turn, Elisian charged down the back chute and attempted to out-brake Rathmann going into turn three. Instead, he lost control, sliding up into Rathmann's car.

Just behind them, Jimmy Reece stood on his brakes and turned sideways in the groove, setting off a chaotic chain-reaction of spinning and wrecking among the majority of the cars behind him. Popular Pat O'Connor lost his life when his car ran over the wheel of another machine, flipped, and burst into flames. Jerry Unser was launched into a pin-wheeling somersault over the fence and suffered a dislocated shoulder.

When the American contingent returned to Italy for the second Monza 500-miler, Ward made the trip as a participant. But after qualifying ninth for the first heat, a broken torsion bar sidelined the Wolcott Fuel Injection Special after only 16 laps. Though repaired for the second event of the three scheduled, the car continued to have mechanical problems, and Ward retired it after 31 additional circuits. Jim Rathmann won all three heats and claimed the top prize for Watson and the John Zink team.

Returning from Europe seemed to allow the Wolcott team to turn things around. Just two weeks before the June 29 race at Monza, Rodger had been too slow to make the show at Langhorne, yet on the 4th of July, he was second fastest qualifier at Atlanta. Rodger led the first 48 laps before pitting during a caution period to replace a worn right front tire. Then he had to fight his way back to collect seventh at the finish.

The next race was the 200-miler at Milwaukee, which had become one of Rodger's favorite tracks. Starting from the ninth slot, he took the lead from pole qualifier Jim Rathmann, who was in the Zink roadster, on lap 14. They traded the lead three more times before Rodger went in front for good on lap 61 and paced the remaining 140 miles.

Rodger's second win of the season came on another paved mile, Trenton. He qualified the Wolcott roadster on the outside of the front row and led every lap. With a big lead, he was the first car to take the checkers as Jimmy Reece lost control in the first turn, while battling Johnny Thomson for second,

Indy 1958. A pileup in the third turn of the first lap eliminated many of the cars. Rodger navigated his way through the melee. While cars slowly drive past the cleanup, emergency workers continue to put out the fuel fire on Pat O'Connor's car. In the foreground, Elisian's No. 5 had minimal damage, but Dick Rathmann's 97 was cut in half. *IMS Photo*

and hurtled out of the park. Thrown free when the car broke into several pieces, Reece was dead on the scene.

During the month between Milwaukee and Trenton, Ward had finished fourth twice, at DuQuoin and Syracuse, and third in the Hoosier Hundred. He also raced an Alfa Romeo in a USAC-sanctioned sports car event at Lime Rock. Then in October, Rodger practiced a 4.4-liter Ferrari for the Los Angeles Times Grand Prix, but the clutch failed before qualifying. It was a new challenge for Indy racers, being pitted against top names from the sporty-car contingent, and there was a wide gulf between the two factions. More importantly, however, sports car races offered another payday.

As in the past, the season finished with races in the western part of the country, while the East Coast was preparing for the holidays. Rodger set second quickest qualifying time at Sacramento's mile to earn his seventh top-five start of the year. Once again he grabbed the lead at the green flag and led the first 38 circuits. But this time it was the fuel pump that let him down, and after completing 54 laps he was scored 16th.

Roger Wolcott suffered a heart attack and died on November 1, 1958. Herb Porter packed the team and headed back to Indianapolis. Rodger returned to Phoenix for the season's finale. He found a ride in the Joe Silnes-fabricated Hoover Motor Express dirt-machine, which had earlier been raced by Don Branson and Earl Motter, and qualified it seventh. With a steady

Left: While chief steward Harlan Fengler observes, Rodger is pit-side in the Wolcott roadster. After car owner Roger Wolcott passed away unexpectedly late in the year, the team was operated as a memorial to him in 1959. *IMS Photo*

Right: Jimmy Bryan and Rodger may be talking about Bryan's super-fast waterskiing boat. They raced against each other for more than a decade, both won Indy, and were good friends away from the track. *Steve Zautke Collection*

race, he brought it home fifth, as Tony Bettenhausen clinched the national championship with a second place finish. Tony began the season in the Hardwood Door team's Kurtis, and finished driving for John Zink. He hadn't won a race all season, but earned the title with an amazing record of finishing 10 of the 13 races in the top five.

Although the Wolcott team would continue to race with Herb Porter's leadership, Rodger went looking for a better opportunity. He had come through a significant phase of his career and his life. As a professional racer, he had been dangerously close to the bottom, but had worked himself back to victory lane. It may have taken longer than it took others, but he had established himself as more than just a lead-foot who could wear out a race car. He was a racer who could bring the trophy home when he had the right tools.

Rodger's first race with Leader Card Racing at Daytona in 1959. He has a new Watson chassis and the sun is shining. After finishing second in the USAC National Championship race, he spun in the Formula Libre event and scuffed the wall. Touching the wall with one of A. J's roadsters happened only one other time during all the years he raced with Leader Card. *Cal Lane Collection*

Chapter 5

The Flying W's

Frequently, the future is shaped as much during the off-season as it is on the racetracks. John Zink Jr. had fumed after Dick Rathmann's Watson-built roadster out-qualified Reece and Elisian for the pole at Indy in 1958. Watson had taken the car to Indy unsold and found a buyer in Lee Elkins. Floyd Trevis, Elkins' capable mechanic, then orchestrated Rathmann's pole run. Zink didn't like Watson building cars to sell to competitors and, as the summer continued, told A. J. to relocate from California to Tulsa, Oklahoma, to be nearer to the Zink ranch. This very nearly happened.

At Monza in 1958, Bob Wilke, a long-time midget owner who wanted to become involved with Indy cars, had provided sponsorship for the Zink car Jim Rathmann drove to victory. At the time, Wilke advised Watson, "If you ever need a job, call me."

As he prepared to move to Tulsa, Watson bristled at the thought of working under Zink's close scrutiny. He had secured two Indy wins, the victory at Monza, and the national championship for Zink. Furthermore, he considered the proceeds from the cars he built to be an important part of his income. He told close friends that Zink was just jacking him around, and he knew that in Oklahoma he'd be more controlled by "the farmer" than ever. So, as the 1958 season wore down, he made a phone call to Wisconsin.

Wilke told Watson, "I've got $50,000 and I'm going to spend it this year and go racing." When they met halfway between Milwaukee and Chicago, Wilke brought a station wagon and two Offy engines for Watson. When the championship tour reached DuQuoin in September, Watson informed Zink he had changed his mind and wouldn't be moving. He began work on Wilke's Leader Card team, while Zink and Denny Moore were left to field cars for Tony Bettenhausen in the season's final events.

"I just didn't want to go to Tulsa," Watson said. "We had decided to go and had sold our house in California. Out there [in Oklahoma] we didn't even have a place to live. Then we had to quick buy another house when I decided to quit Zink."

1959

When Rodger heard that Bob Wilke and A. J. Watson were starting a new team, he contacted Wilke. Watson's first choice for a driver had been Jim Rathmann, and he was nearly signed, but ultimately he changed his mind and decided to drive for Jack Beckley on Lindsey Hopkins' team. Watson then tried to hire George Amick, but Amick elected to go to a new Quinn Epperly–built lay-down being fielded by Bob Bowes of Bowes Seal Fast and George Bignotti. Ward kept calling Wilke, and it finally paid off.

"Wilke wasn't talking to me much about it; it was strictly Wilke," Watson recalls. "He knew drivers probably better than I did because he went to a lot of races. He [Ward] was real popular; running midgets he was real popular. That might have been one of the reasons that he hired Ward, I don't know."

Watson began building a new roadster and a dirt car in preparation for the series opener. As it had been the year before, the first race was in April, but this time it was at the new 2½-mile Daytona International Speedway, which had just hosted the first Daytona 500.

The $50,000 that Wilke mentioned in his phone call proved to be Watson's budget, for that year and several more that

Above: Qualifying at Indy completed, Rodger and the crew are pleased with sixth starting position. *Armin Krueger*

Left: Rodger receives congratulations from Bob Wilke (left) and A. J. Watson (leaning against car on right) after his qualifying run. *Armin Krueger*

Opposite: From left to right, Dick Rathmann, Jim Rathmann, Ward, Dempsey Wilson, Elmer George, and Bob Christie fill the first three rows of the opening race at Daytona. After this day, Indy cars would never return to the high-banked Speedway. *Cal Lane Collection*

Basement Bessie

With a career that paralleled Rodger's chronologically for many years, Watson got his start by building roadsters that raced near his Glendale, California, home after returning from the Air Corps where he had trained to be a navigator. In 1947, Andy Granatelli's Hurricane Racing series drew A. J. and several of his racing cronies—including Pat Flaherty and the Rathmann brothers—to Chicago. Then, an unplanned visit to Indy gave his life a new direction. "In '48, a friend of mine was building a car for Bob Estes for the Speedway and needed a spare engine brought back," he recalls. "My buddy had a nice big Chrysler and we put this Ford flathead engine in the trunk and brought her back to him. That was the first race I'd seen and I got hooked on it."

The only way Watson knew to become involved with the Speedway was to build his own car. Typical of his usual approach, he forged ahead by the seat of his pants. When the next May rolled around, he showed up with a hand-built racer, using pieces from a variety of sources. The construction was so basic and the parts so common that after being inspected,

it was referred to as *Basement Bessie*. Watson brought his buddy, Flaherty, to drive. With both of them being rookies, it wasn't surprising they didn't make the race.

In 1950, A. J. returned with a car that was largely financed by a variety of friends in his hometown of Glendale, California. Although formally named the City of Glendale Special, the white and blue machine was affectionately nicknamed the *Pots and Pan Spl*. With Dick Rathmann at the wheel, they qualified for the race but were sidelined by an early engine problem.

When car owner Bob Estes purchased the *Pots and Pan Spl.*, he hired Watson and Jud Phillips as the mechanics. In 1953, Estes had them build a new car for Don Freeland. Three years later, A. J. was hired by Zink to operate his new team. At just 29 years old, Watson won his first Indy 500 and national title. The next year he won Indy again, this time with a roadster he designed and built. By 1959, A. J. could pretty much write his own ticket, a fact John Zink seemed to overlook when he tried to strong-arm the independently-minded Californian.

followed. "Wilke didn't spend a lot of money," Watson recalled. "When we first started, we were like a super-team, but we only spent $50,000 a year. That wouldn't even touch what they were using later on in our career. I had to do all of the engines, and most people hired their engines out. We just didn't hire enough help to get it all done.

"I always had guys out there work for me but I never paid them. The guys worked at Lockheed and when they got off work, they'd come down and have a few beers. And the more beers you gave them the longer they worked and the harder they worked. I always had a lot of free help out there," Watson said. He added that Rodger's deal with Wilke paid $500 a race, plus 40 percent of whatever they won. If he won the race, Rodger collected 50 percent.

"He was giving me 20 percent of the purse, too, which was too much," said A. J. "He finally cut that down after we won the Speedway. He said he couldn't give me 20 percent anymore, because he didn't have anything left for himself. He cut it down to 17 percent, but that was still good."

The introduction of USAC's national championship division to Daytona was a rough experience. Just two months before the first championship race, veteran Marshall Teague was killed trying to set a world speed record on the new oval in the Sumar streamliner that Jimmy Daywalt had driven without the fenders and canopy at Indy in 1955. Given the recent experience of racing at Monza, USAC had concerns about the ability of the typical championship trail car to withstand the pounding the cars normally experienced, combined with the G-forces of the high-speed banks. The result was that USAC reduced the national championship event to 100 miles and added a 100-mile Formula Libre (run what you brung) non-points race, which it hoped would lure Grand Prix and sports cars to compete against the Indy roadsters.

Jerry Unser, oldest of the three racing brothers and who had 10 starts in national championship racing, was given the opportunity to wring out the new Leader Card dirt car. But Unser didn't make it to qualifying. As A. J. remembered, "The racetrack was built with real sharp edges at the bottom, and

Above: A. J. Watson's crew was usually made up of the fellows who helped in his California race shop. The 70 seconds Rodger spent in the pits at Indianapolis was an average of 4 seconds better time per stop than Rathmann's stops. *Armin Krueger*

Left: Johnny Thomson is chasing Ward at Indy. Thomson led 40 laps and may have had a faster car, but four pit stops kept him from challenging late in the race. *Author Collection*

he lost it and hit that bump; he never flipped, never hit the fence, but he bent the shit out of it and we had to park it."

Dick Rathmann was the top qualifier, putting the Sumar Kurtis-Kraft on the pole at 173.210 miles per hour. Rodger timed the new Leader Card Watson roadster third, led five laps, and finished second. Jim Rathmann, the elder of the brothers, dominated the race in the other new Watson chassis, averaging 170.2 miles per hour for the victory.

Describing the excitement of winning his first 500, Rodger said, "Now, I wouldn't want you to think that I was a little confused at my first win, but as we got toward the end of the race, I kept thinking, 'Well, how many more laps are there?' Then we had the white flag and I said, 'Okay, you idiot, don't crash it now. I mean, you've got it won.' I got the checkered flag and I thought, 'Well, they might have miscounted. I'd better run one more lap just to be damn sure.' So I ran one more lap and then I couldn't remember where Victory Lane was." *Gene Crucean Collection*

On the last lap, "Little George" Amick, who had turned the fastest lap at 176.887 in the second qualifying round, got the new Bowes out of the draft while passing Bob Christie in turn two and lost control. Bill Cheesbourg later reported, "He started flipping and I had to spin to keep from hitting him. As I was sliding backwards—they counted 2,200 feet—he was flipping alongside me" (Wallen 1993). Amick, who had already scored three championship victories and was considered one of the best of the young chargers, died instantly.

With the time spent clearing the debris, the second race was shortened to just 20 laps. Rodger started third, as the lineup was based on the same qualifying times, and again took the early lead, passing Jim on the second circuit. But two laps later, Ward spun in turn two and lightly touched the wall. Rathmann led the rest of the way for his second victory of the day.

Rodger's first opportunity to drive the repaired Leader Card Duo dirt car came at Trenton two weeks later. Rodger qualified seventh and was up to second in just 20 laps. He battled Bettenhausen every trip around the paved mile, leading lap 26, being re-passed on lap 27, then moving ahead again on lap 35. After 14 circuits on Ward's tail, Bettenhausen fought back into the lead. Don Branson, running third, spun while working lapped cars and trapped Dick Linder on the outside. Linder's car catapulted over the third turn fence and he became the third fatality of the season. The race was finally flagged because of rain on lap 89, with Rodger still on Bettenhausen's tail.

The Indianapolis Motor Speedway opened for practice a few weeks later and, as May progressed, Rodger was full of optimism. He and Rathmann traded the top seat on the speed chart, and one day both registered identical 144.555 laps. Things were going so smoothly that one day Rodger shook down the

Left: Rodger on his first Victory Lane ceremony at Indy: "Now, I want you to know that I wasn't excited or nervous or anything like that, but I could not actually remember where Victory Lane was. So I came down and they were waving at me, 'Over here! Over here!' So obviously I drove it over there. They showed me the newspaper, and I didn't know how they knew I was going to win." *IMS Photo*

Below: The Leader Card crew is excited over the victory. Most of them had been working on the new cars throughout the winter. Larry Shinoda, holding the newspaper declaring Ward's victory aloft, became a noted autobile designer. His credits includes the Cherolet Corvette and Ford Boss Mustang. *IMS Photo*

Leader Card Duo dirt car, which had been entered presumably to provide more garage space but also served as a backup. Then the next day he helped set up Agajanian's Kuzma roadster and coached rookie Chuck Daigh. Dick Rathmann and Tony Bettenhausen joined the speed chase and, as pole day approached, Johnny Thomson raised the ante with a 146.2 circuit in the new pink Racing Associates sidewinder out of Lesovsky's shop.

Thomson captured the pole, with Eddie Sachs and Jim Rathmann filling the front row. The second row included Dick Rathmann and Bobby Grim on Rodger's left, as he had the outside slot. His qualifying time of 144.035 had been only seventh fastest, nearly 2 miles per hour off of Thomson's speed.

In his eight previous starts, Rodger had only run the distance once, finishing eighth in 1956, which was also his only top-10 finish. In a race preview, *Sports Illustrated* failed to mention

Victory Lane is a busy place. Years later, Rodger remembered, "We had a lovely movie star, Miss Erin O'Brien. That was kind of a pleasant part of the ceremony when we got a little kiss, and I enjoyed it so much I thought I'd go back for seconds. I had her kind of bent back over the car and she was squirming a little bit. Then I realized she was leaning pretty close to the exhaust pipe, which may have been the cause. I thought it was me." *Rodger Ward Jr.*

Above left: It finally all came together. Rodger is dirty and grimy, Jo is hugging him, he has the bottle of milk, and the Borg Warner Trophy is on the Watson. *IMS Photo*

Above right: Weariness from the pressure and emotion of race day can be seen on the faces. Rodger and Jo have finally made it back to the garage. *IMS Photo*

Left: Rodger takes a couple of quiet minutes to relax with A. J. after the race. "Well, how did it go today?" they could be asking each other. *IMS Photo*

him at all, and William F. Fox of the *Indianapolis News* ranked Ward's odds at 9:1, just behind Thomson and Jim Rathmann. Yet optimism is frequently a matter of perspective, and neither *Sports Illustrated* nor Bill Fox was sitting in the shiny white No. 5 roadster with A. J. and his gang working the pits. Thus, the day before the 500, when a reporter asked if he'd trade running the race for second place money right then, Rodger declined. He knew that this was the opportunity he had been waiting for his whole life.

When the green flag sent the 33 starters on their 500-mile journey, Rodger took just one lap to work past Sachs and the

One of the traditions of the Indianapolis 500 is the official photo session for the winner on the morning after the race. *Armin Krueger*

Rathmann brothers into second behind Thomson. He closed in on the pink car and passed Thomson in the first turn on the fifth circuit. Then Jim Rathmann joined the battle while Flaherty hustled up from 18th starting spot, making it a tight four-car pack. Running laps at over 140 miles per hour, the action looked like a Saturday night trophy dash. Before they had run 50 laps, all four had taken turns in the lead and were starting to pit.

After a pair of caution flags—one for Sutton's wall smacker and a four-car tangle featuring Mike Magill's flip in turn three, plus another for the leader's pit stops—Thomson and Ward were at the head of the field and began to set a blistering pace. On lap 84, Thomson made his second pit stop, taking 35 seconds, but Ward didn't have to pit until almost 20 laps later.

Above left: Rodger and Jo sit for a winner's portrait. Rodger explained what it meant to be an Indy winner: "Indy makes the race driver. You become famous when you come here. I don't care where else you race in the world, and I've raced all over the world. I came here the first year in 1951. I was pretty famous in my own territory, but after I came to Indianapolis I wasn't known as a driver from California. I was an Indy driver. That really—for me, that was prestige. It took me a little while to win the race, but when I finally did get into the right equipment, God, it was unbelievable. The experience of winning here, I can't describe to you how wonderful it was." *IMS Photo*

Above right: Rodger with Jim Rathmann. After winning the season opener, Rathmann was shut out the rest of the season. Rodger won four times and earned the national championship. Asked what Indy winners talk about when they get together, he replied, "Well, we lie to each other a little about how great we were, and how come we won that race and what were you doing? I don't know, it's a very select group of people." *Rodger Ward Jr.*

This page and opposite: Opportunities increase greatly once you win Indy and they all help put beans on the table. When Rodger and Tony Bettenhausen raced a match race in midgets at Illiana Speedway, Rodger took the win. This sequence shows the two cars ready to be pushed off, Tony and Rodger racing wheel-to-wheel, and the legendary Tinley Park Express congratulating Rodger after the race. *Ken Coles*

Left: Rodger, short track veteran Al Miller (left), and starter Bill Vandewater (center). Miller, whose real name was Albert Krulock, raced at Indianapolis four times. Vandewater was the chief starter at the Speedway for eight years and became known for flagging midget races at 16th Street Speedway the night before, then flagging at the 500 the next morning. *Ken Coles*

Above: Three Indy 500 champions: Rodger with Sam Hanks (1957) and Jimmy Bryan (1958). Hanks announced his retirement in Victory Lane, 1957, and afterwards served as Director of Racing at the Speedway. Bryan lost his life at Langhorne. *Dick Wallen Collection*

When his time came, Watson refueled the car, changed the right front and both rear tires, and sent Rodger back onto the track in just 23 seconds, so he didn't lose the lead.

Rodger led the rest of the race. Back on the leader's lap after Ward's stop, Rathmann began to close the gap. At one point during a caution flag, Watson signaled to Ward, "*He's cheating!*" But Rodger maintained a 4.5 second advantage until Rathmann had to make his third pit stop and fell behind

Thomson. Running laps at 144 miles per hour, Rodger built a lead of nearly a full minute. When Flaherty hit the wall coming off turn four, partially blocking the pit road entrance, Rodger threaded the needle and visited Watson for his final change of tires and fuel.

At 2:46 p.m., Rodger raced under Bill Vandewater's checkered flag, his right fist raised in jubilation, and 23 seconds later, Rathmann finished second for the third time in his career.

Coming to the green in the Milwaukee 100, Thomson on the pole (3), Ward outside, Boyd (88), and Foyt (10). Thomson, Boyd, and Foyt finished 1-2-3, while Rodger's engine blew after 98 laps. *Armin Krueger photo, Gene Crucean Collection*

On his way to the 1959 National Championship, Rodger won twice in the Leader Card Duo dirt car, at DuQuoin and the Indiana State Fairgrounds. Both came after Jim Bryan lost his life in the same car. *IMS Photo*

Thomson was 27 seconds further back. When interviewed over the public address, Rathmann admitted, "I charged as hard as I could, but I just didn't make it."

In Victory Lane, Watson, the crew, Bob Wilke, Jo, and their dog, Skippy, all greeted Ward. When movie star Erin O'Brien moved in for the celebratory kiss, Rodger warned, "My face is dirty."

"I don't care, if you don't," she replied.

Several factors contributed greatly to the victory. Rodger had been able to stay with Thomson when the pole-sitter built a sizeable lead shortly before mid-race, which resulted in a huge advantage when Thomson had to pit some 20 minutes earlier than Ward.

The pit work of Watson's crew was clearly another of the deciding factors. All told, Rodger spent 70 seconds in the pits, compared to Rathmann's 82 seconds. The fast pit work was aided by air jacks, which Watson had installed on the cars over the winter, that lifted the car when a nitrogen hose was attached.

Left: Old-time racers, like Watson, frequently associate a team with a specific chief mechanic. Today, A. J. associates the Wolcott team with Herb Porter. Watson didn't have a high opinion of Ward until they started to work together at Leader Card. "He just settled down. He was kind of a bum until we hired him. He was hanging out in the bars like a lot of people did back then. He just never did get a steady ride, until he drove for Herb Porter. He did good in Herb Porter's car. Not at the Speedway, but on the miles he ran real good. And then we hired him from Wolcott. He just caught on and did good. I think he was right. He had that Porter ride, but they were having trouble and he was getting kind of hungry. That helps sometimes." *IMS*

Left: During the fair week in August, Rodger captured victories in the USAC stock car race and the 100-lap midget race leading up to the national championship race. *IMS*

August 30, 1959, Milwaukee 200. Rodger working the outside, lapping Dick Rathmann in the Hardwood Doors Kurtis (25). Johnny Boyd in Bowes Seal Fast 33 chasing. Ward started 19th and took the lead on lap 62.
Armin Krueger photo, Gene Crucean Collection

Although Thomson may have had the fastest car, he pitted early and made four stops to the three of Ward and Rathmann, which ultimately took him out of contention for the win.

Rodger said, "On the first stop, I made the mistake of taking a deep breath or two before reaching for a cup of water and a pair of clean goggles. I didn't get either, because Watson tapped me on the helmet and said 'go' at the same time. But I was ready for such fast service on my other two stops." When it was out of the pit crews' hands, Rodger kept the pressure on, turning fast laps whether working through traffic or running alone, and never gave Rathmann a chance to close within striking distance.

"He ran hard all day, he didn't do much stroking," Watson commented. While it was Watson's third Indy win in five years, it was the first for Bob and Rodger. At the next night's victory banquet, the winner's payoff came to $106,850 for the new Leader Card Racing team.

Winning Indy also takes luck. Later, when tearing the engine down, Watson found that the piston pin plug, holding the number two piston in position for proper clearance, had worked loose and broken the oil ring, as well as one of the two compression rings.

"It had aluminum plugs on each end of the Offy. Once in a while they would wear the button out and then you'd cut a groove in the cylinder wall," A. J. explained. It was inevitable that the other compression ring would also fail under the strain—but it had held long enough for Ward to drive 500 miles.

With a 200-point lead in the championship, Ward and Watson headed to Milwaukee. Starting next to Thomson on the front row, Rodger chased the Pennsylvanian for 98 laps until his Offy expired. Stating an aversion to Langhorne, the Indy winner skipped it without losing any ground in the standings.

In July, Rodger was back in a midget, this time at the quarter-mile Illiana Speedway in Schererville, Indiana. In a highly publicized match race featuring the new Indianapolis champion, he outran Tony Bettenhausen, one of the drivers he looked up to the most. He then went on to win the night's feature,

Above left: Rodger led the last 41 laps to claim the win in the Milwaukee 200. Victory Lane never gets old. *IMS Photo*

Above right: Rodger in Victory Lane after the Milwaukee 200. He dropped out of four national championship races in 1959. In the other events, he had five wins, was runner-up twice, and third twice. *IMS Photo*

Below left: Rodger in victory lane with Jo and the Wilkes at Milwaukee. Winning at Bob Wilke's home track was special, as he had been a sponsor of the races for many years. *Armin Krueger*

Below right: The spoils after winning the midget race on the Milwaukee Mile, Rodger receives awards from Hoosier Auto Racing Fans (HARF) members. *C. V. Haschel photo, Author Collection*

Thanks to Jo

Breaking down preconceived judgments was much more difficult back then than it is today. Leader Card Racing brought a winning pedigree and top equipment. Rodger had shown he could win on the circuit. Plus, he had dramatically changed his lifestyle. Yet the damage of years spent at the wheel of marginal equipment, while forging a troublesome reputation and fueling it with an obstinate attitude, could ruin the career of a driver in the 1950s. Some remained unconvinced that Rodger had what it took to become a top racer. Even after winning the 500, there were those who, like Floyd Clymer, publisher of the *Floyd Clymer's Indianapolis 500 Mile Race Yearbook*, admitted to being surprised.

In the introduction to Clymer's 1959 yearbook, he wrote, "Uncertainty is, of course, one of the things that makes automobile racing interesting. However, few, including myself, felt that Rodger Ward would be the winner.

"I had always figured Rodger as a consistent, capable driver, but one who, in view of his past record at Indianapolis, wasn't destined to win the 500, even though all of his performances have been worthwhile. . . . I had figured Rodger good for about third, fourth, or fifth place, if he had no trouble."

Rodger confided to *Indianapolis Star* Sports Editor Jep Cadou, "The fact that my wife has stood behind me, and beside me, and boosted my morale when I needed it, helped me a great deal. There were a lot of times when it was a little rough to figure out what we were going to eat, but she never complained. She deserves as much credit as anyone."

While Ward was racing at Williams Grove, Bettenhausen drove Ward's Ford to victory in the USAC stock car race in Milwaukee.

Less than 60 days after Indy, Connecticut's 1 1/2-mile Lime Rock road course, in association with USAC, promoted a Formula Libre event on July 25. Unable to arrange a ride in a sports car, Ward agreed to drive Ken Brenn's midget, a 12-year-old Kurtis-Kraft/Offy—the 1958 American Racing Drivers Club (ARDC) champion—against many of the top sports car racers in the nation. Brock Yates of *Car and Driver* called it "the first shot in a major revolution that would turn U. S. road racing upside down." (November 1999)

The formidable competition included: George Constantine's 4.2-liter DBR2 Aston Martin; a 2.5-liter 250F Maserati driven by Chuck Daigh (the same car that Juan Manuel Fangio drove to victory in the German Grand Prix at the Nürburgring two years earlier); a Maserati 300S; Cooper Formula 2 Climax; Cooper Monaco; Corvette Sting Ray; Ferraris; Jaguars; Porsches; and more. Against all of them, Rodger qualified almost a second faster than any of the others, setting a new record.

But Ward ran second to Constantine in the first 20-lap heat race. "We were running a gear that was a little bit too low," he said. "So between heats I said, 'Guys, bump that ratio up by about 20 points. That will solve this problem.' We didn't have a clutch. We put it in gear and went. You have to understand that a midget is a tremendously versatile race car. It would go like hell. The only problem I had in the first heat was that I was over-winding the engine and I had to back off on the long front straightaway."

Brenn's crew went to work on the Kurtis, installing a taller gear and adjusting the torsion bars. The second heat began

besting Shorty Templeman. Two days later, he claimed a victory in Williams Grove Speedway's annual non-points champ car race. The night was marred by the tragic death of Van Johnson, who was coming off his first victory in a national event, having won at Langhorne.

After breaking the track's qualifying record and starting on the pole, Rodger led until rain halted the racing after 13 laps.

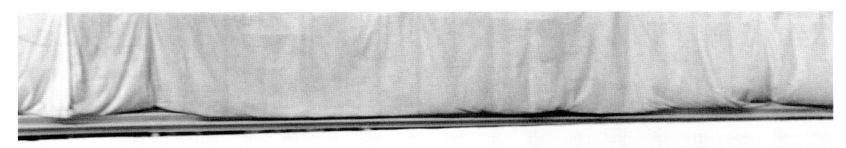

Above left: Rodger led every lap and beat Don Branson and Tony Bettenhausen in the Ted Horn 100 at DuQuoin Fairgrounds. *C. V. Haschel photo, Author Collection*

Above: A midget veteran, Gene Hartley followed his father's footsteps throughout his career. However, Gene ran 32 championship races over 12 years, including 10 Indianapolis starts, while Ted Hartley didn't make it onto the championship trail. *Ken Coles*

Left: Bobby Grim was a champion on the International Motor Contest Association (IMCA) sprint car circuit before joining the championship tour in 1958. His only victory came at Syracuse, New York, in 1960, driving a dirt car owned by Bill Forbes and built by Wally Meskowski. *Ken Coles*

with a stirring dice between the Aston Martin and the chalky-blue midget, then Rodger was able to pull away and win by three seconds.

When the concluding 90-mile finale took the green, Rodger grabbed the lead with Constantine and Daigh in close pursuit. Each took a turn in the lead before the Aston Martin fell out

Rodger in Ken Brenn's Kurtis-Kraft/Offy. It was the American Racing Drivers Club (ARDC) championship car. Few changes were made before the race, and it only had a single speed gearbox. Between the heats, the crew changed the gear which gave Rodger a little more top end speed on the straightaway. *Rodger Ward Jr.*

with a wheel bearing failure. By 30 laps, Ward and Daigh were locked in a close battle and were the only cars left on the lead lap. Then, as the brakes on the heavier Maserati became vulnerable, Rodger pulled slowly away to command a full straightaway lead at the finish. Two other midgets—one wheeled by Bert Brooks, and the Caruso midget with Russ Klar and Tony Bettenhausen sharing the driving duties—also scored top-10 finishes. They trailed Daigh, who held on for the runner-up position, Pedro Rodriguez in another Maserati, John Fitch, and Constantine.

Rodger kicked off Fair Week at the historic Milwaukee Mile with a victory in the 150-lap stock car event on Sunday, August 23, just a day after dropping out of Springfield's 100-miler with a burned piston. Thursday's mid-week 200-mile stock car event was rained out, but on Saturday he pushed Wilke's midget to victory lane in the 100-mile midget race.

On an oily track, Rodger went out to qualify for Sunday's national championship race, but only managed a 10th row seat. He was working steadily to the front, when Foyt's engine blew in the first turn. Everyone missed the oil for two laps, but Ed Elisian got into it on his third time past, lost control, and slammed into the wall. The Travelon Trailer roadster rolled upside down and, when the fuel tank split, burst into flames. It was a gruesome scene, as the fire burned for nine minutes with Elisian trapped in the car.

When racing resumed, Rodger continued his march to the front, taking the lead from Bettenhausen on lap 62. Bettenhausen went back in front 11 laps later and held it until lap 160, when he tried to clean the windscreen with a rag. When the rag slipped and blew back into his face as he was setting up for turn three, he spun out. It was the third consecutive year that Rodger captured a championship series victory at Milwaukee, but Elisian's death subdued any celebration.

Rodger scored his first dirt track win with the Leader Card Duo at DuQuoin's annual Labor Day event. Starting outside the front row, he beat Don Branson to the first turn and led the rest of the way. This gave him a 520-point lead over Thomson, with just five races remaining. Then six days later, Thomson was thrown from his flipping sprint car at Williams Grove and suffered injuries that would sideline him for the rest of the season. With Rodger's third place at Syracuse the afternoon before, the national crown was virtually assured.

Above: Chasing George Constantine in the Aston-Martin DB2R. Rodger called the victory a great thrill, but most likely his biggest thrill was whipping the "strokers and brokers" in their own backyard. *Gordon White*

Right: This is the plaque that Rodger was awarded for the victory at Lime Rock. The inscription reads, "Lime Rock, Intn'l. Form. Libre, July '59, Best Performance By Amer. Track Race Car, Presented To _____, By Dr. R. N. Sabourin." Some doodad that was originally glued on the plaque is missing and Rodger's name was never added. Nothing, that day, was more amateurish than this award. *Rodger Ward Jr.*

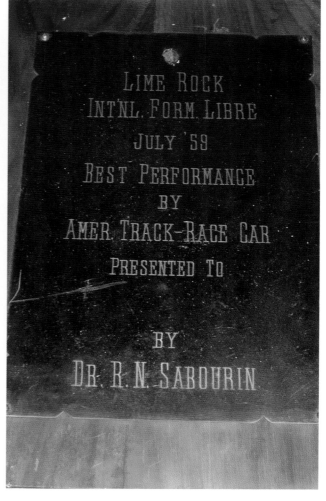

The rookie team mathematically secured the national championship the next weekend at the Hoosier Hundred. Rodger claimed his first pole in nearly two years (second when counting the non-points event at Williams Grove). He led each of the 100-laps as Eddie Sachs took second from Foyt. Subbing for the injured Thomson, Jim Hurtubise finished 16th in his first national championship race after getting snarled with Bettenhausen and Sutton.

In theory, with his victories at Indianapolis and Lime Rock, Rodger rated a better ride than a midget for the Los Angeles Times Grand Prix at Riverside in October. Driving Bob Sorrel's 4.4-liter Ferrari, which was described as a diabolically evil chassis with a hairy, thoroughly unreliable engine, Rodger qualified only 28th, but managed to win the consolation heat (Wallen 2000). But Dan Gurney's Ferrari stalled at the green flag and collected Jack Graham, who then ricocheted into Ward as he attempted to dodge past, thus all three were eliminated.

It had been the best season of Rodger's career, perhaps the best year of his life. The Leader Card team had earned five wins, including the Indianapolis 500. Bettenhausen's pair of victories edged Thomson for second in the standings by 30 points, and both Rathmann and Sachs had also won twice.

1960

Rodger started the new year testing Firestone tires at the Speedway with Bettenhausen and Thomson, who had recovered

Left: Rodger was invited to race in the U.S. Grand Prix at Sebring and brought the Leader Card midget. Watson and the crew installed a clutch, transmission, and two-speed gearbox before leaving for Florida. *Cal Lane Collection*

Below: "Now, I've got to tell you that the cars in that era were somewhat less respectable than today's Formula 1 cars, but it was a lot of fun," said Rodger. "Finally I had trouble. I had to put a clutch in the car, and a midget with a clutch and a transmission is somewhat handicapped. I finally lost the clutch and had to stop in the race and that was probably a good thing. But I had a world of fun and met a lot of great guys." *Rodger Ward Jr.*

Opposite top left: Jayne Mansfield was one of the celebrity guests at the Speedway for the 1961 race. Here, she and Rodger pose for a publicity shot before the Victory Banquet. *IMS Photo*

Opposite top right: When Tony Bettenhausen (shown) was killed at Indianapolis, Eddie Sachs admitted, "I saw Tony heading for the wall. I watched until it was over. Then I sat down and cried like a baby." *Ken Coles*

Opposite bottom left: May 1960; Rodger receives the "Baby Borg" Borg-Warner Trophy for winning the 1959 Indianapolis 500. This is a traditional part of the next year's drivers' meeting. *IMS Photo*

Opposite bottom right: Wilke (left) and Watson (right) in the pits at Indy, 1960. Watson once explained how he got hooked up with Wilke: "I got to know Wilke when he sponsored Zink's car for Monza. We went over to Monza and won the race over there. Wilke had told me over there that if I ever needed a job, to call him. That's how, when Zink jacked me around a little bit, I called him and he said meet me in Chicago and we'll set up a deal." *Armin Krueger*

Left: Eddie Sachs (left) with Clint Brawner (next to Sachs) in the garage area after the pole qualifying run in 1960. Sachs led 21 laps before dropping out with a magneto failure after 132 laps. *Ken Coles*

Below left: The front row starters, Rodger, Jim Rathmann, and Sachs clown around with a couple of go-karts during a photo session for the press. Rathmann was marketing the karts. *Author Collection*

from his injuries; then he headed to Trenton for the season opener. Thomson captured the pole, but Rodger started his season right by grabbing the lead from outside of the front row and keeping Tony behind him. Although he led every lap, it wasn't boring. A week later, Ward and Bettenhausen joined Foyt, Sachs, Branson, and Jim McWithey at Langhorne to shoot a pilot for a proposed television series. Driving the Ray Brady Kurtis 4000, Rodger was the slowest of the bunch and didn't make the 10-lap feature, which was won by Branson. That was as close as television came to hosting a weekly show based on USAC's championship division in the 1960s.

Rodger's momentum carried to Indianapolis and, for the first time in his career, he qualified for the front row. He was in a new Watson roadster, as was Jim Rathmann, who started between Ward and pole-winner Eddie Sachs. Watson had been overwhelmed with orders for new cars during the winter, so he provided a set of plans to fabricator Wayne Ewing. Sachs' Dean

Grand Prix drive

Lured by a big enough financial incentive, Rodger and A. J. took Wilke's midget to Sebring's U.S. Grand Prix on December 12, 1959. In preparation for this road course that was built on an airport, they had installed a clutch, two-speed transmission, and rear end, and the car had been renumbered to "1." But the benefits that the midget had provided at Lime Rock were overwhelmed by Sebring's 5.2-mile layout. Another disadvantage was that they had to run the Offy on gasoline in accordance with the Grand Prix rules. During the weekend, Rodger developed friendships with several of the Grand Prix drivers, including Jack Brabham, who had cut his teeth in New Zealand's midgets, and British racing champion Stirling Moss.

"For a while I was running pretty good, seventh or eighth in the race," Rodger recalled. "I was ahead of the Porsches and a goodly number of the mediocre cars. Of course the really true Formula 1 cars, they were gone. But that didn't matter to me, I just kept going. Finally I looked over at my right rear tire and it was through the cord, and I thought, 'Oh, shit, I've got to stop.' So I did." The Wilke midget was officially retired with a clutch failure.

Van Lines machine was one of the cars Ewing built. When Wilke wanted to expand the team to two cars, Rodger helped convince Chuck Stevenson, who had limited his racing to stock cars since the wreck at DuQuoin, to drive the second Leader Card machine.

At the green flag, Rodger took advantage of being on the front row, cutting across before the first turn and leading the opening lap. Sachs overtook him and paced two laps before Rodger went back into the lead. By the time Rodger made his first pit stop, he was leading by 10 seconds. When Watson slapped the top of his helmet—the signal to take off—Rodger let out the clutch but forgot to stand on the gas pedal and the car stalled. When he roared out of the pits 40 seconds behind and upset with his mistake, he began pushing hard. Instinctively, Rodger jacked extra weight onto the right side of the car and employed every technique he knew to shave precious 10ths of seconds from each turn.

The lead changed 29 times among Ward, Rathmann, Sachs, Ruttman, and Thomson, breaking the record for the 500. Sachs battled aggressively, leading five times before dropping out with a magneto failure. Troy Ruttman had two periods in the lead before parking the John Zink car with gear failure, and Thomson paced 10 laps. But after the 75th circuit, the race turned into an old-fashioned duel between Rathmann and Ward, who had finally made up the lost time.

On the last stop, Watson got Rodger out of the pits ahead of Rathmann's *Ken-Paul Spl.*, and they traded the lead for the sixth and seventh time. Later, Rodger recalled that with less than 100 miles remaining, he made a tactical decision, "Well, I'm going to put a little distance between me and Rathmann. And I went after it pretty hard."

But Rathmann was probably employing his own tactics and instead of opening a gap, they passed each other several more times. Suddenly, Rodger began to see warning marks on his right front tire and realized that it was wearing a lot faster than it should have, the result of the extra weight he had wedged to that side more than 100 laps earlier. Recognizing that he needed to conserve his tires, he allowed Rathmann back in front and began to slow his pace, anticipating that Jim would also be concerned about his tires and follow suit.

Since he had been able to pass Rathmann coming onto the straightaways from the turns, Rodger was confident that he could retake the lead whenever he wanted. This tactic appeared to be working well until Watson signaled that Thomson, who was in third place, was closing the gap.

If Thomson was closing that quickly, his tires were probably in better condition, Rodger reasoned, and he didn't want to risk a three-car battle. Taking charge, he passed Rathmann and picked up the pace, hoping to baby his tires while keeping Thomson from gaining enough to be able to see them on the straightaways. Then Thomson's engine soured, so he made a stop in the pits and returned with only three cylinders.

With less than 18 miles left, Rodger decided that the time had come to go for the win and took the lead. But too much damage had been done. Rodger later explained, "With three and a half laps to go, the cord came through on the right front tire. I thought he showed very poor sportsmanship to pass a cripple and go on and win the damn race. I mean, what the heck?"

Although Rathmann's tires were nearly as bad, he overtook Rodger while at the same time turning the fastest lap of the race at 146.1 miles per hour. Rodger finished less than 13 seconds

Above: Rodger is in front of the field at Indianapolis, with Rathmann on his tail, on the first lap in 1960. Sachs took the lead on the second circuit. *Armin Krueger*

Left: Many consider Ward's battle with Rathmann one of the greatest Indy 500s in history. *Armin Krueger*

Life and Death

Rodger once spoke about Jimmy Bryan's death at Langhorne.

"Jimmy got killed in my race car at Langhorne, Pennsylvania, in 1960. I wouldn't race at Langhorne—I didn't like the joint. So he came to me and said, 'Rodger, I've been talking to Watson and he says that if it's okay with you, he'll take your dirt car to Langhorne for me to drive.'

"I said, 'You S.O.B., I wish you wouldn't ask. That joint scares the shit out of me.'

"He said, 'You know, Rodger, I've really performed very well up there and won the race several times. I kind of like the joint.'

"And I said, 'But you never drove a four-bar car up there.' I said, 'I don't think that S.O.B. really is the right race car for that racetrack.'

"And he said, 'Oh, I think I'll be alright.' And he promised to be careful. So he goes up there and kills himself.

"That race car! I hated that son of a bitch from then on! It didn't really hurt the race car that much. He got it upside down. Langhorne was a very hazardous racetrack. It was a 1-mile circle and of course it wasn't a true circle, the radius is changing and it always got rough. I wouldn't run there. I ran there, but I said, 'Bullshit! I don't need this bullshit!' There's no reason to go to a racetrack that you're not comfortable on. It makes no sense to me. But he went there and he liked the joint and he won races there. Of course he was a big tough guy. It pissed me off. It pissed me off that he killed himself, but it pissed me off even more that he did it in my race car.

"The car really wasn't hurt that bad. We finished up the season with the car. And then I told Watson, 'I can't stand that fucking race car any more, you're going to have to build me a new dirt car.'"

Opposite top: Chased by Bettenhausen (2) at Milwaukee. Rodger started 11th and didn't take the lead until lap 82. It was his fourth victory on the Milwaukee mile. *Armin Krueger*

Opposite bottom left: Rodger celebrates with Jo, Watson, and Wilke (left) in victory lane after the Milwaukee 150. *Armin Krueger*

Opposite bottom right: One of the memorable public address announcers, Chicago's Ed "Twenty-Grand" Steinbock interviews Rodger after the win at Milwaukee. *Armin Krueger*

behind knowing deep inside that he should have won. Having built both cars, Watson took the finish in stride, allowing, "I don't know what caused [the right front tire to wear out], if he had to drive harder or if I had it set up a little bit too loose in the front and it was pushing too much. So we got second. It could have been worse, I guess. He did a good job."

Starting 11th at Milwaukee a week later, Rodger took the lead from A. J. Foyt on the 82nd lap and scored his fourth win on that mile track. It would be his last open-wheel victory of the season. His only other trip to victory lane that year would come at a rare appearance on the Salem, Indiana, half mile, one of the tracks that composed "The Hills" where Rodger and his Ford won a USAC stock car event.

While at Milwaukee, Jimmy Bryan asked Rodger if he could drive the Leader Card dirt car at Langhorne in two weeks. Rodger said he'd already made plans to skip the race, as he and Rathmann were to make a personal appearance at a Formula Junior event on the parking lot outside Roosevelt Raceway. So, Bryan went to Langhorne and was the second fastest qualifier. But during the race, he caught a rut after grabbing the lead on the first lap, somersaulted high into the air, and came to a stop in the infield. He was dead by the time emergency workers got to him.

Following two wins and a second place finish in the season's first three races, the Leader Card team went into a funk following the death of Bryan. There was a 61-day break in the national championship schedule, allowing Rodger to run the Pikes Peak Hill Climb and Tony Bettenhausen to win a USAC stock car race at Milwaukee in Rodger's 1958 Ford.

After he couldn't find the qualifying speed and became a spectator at Springfield, Rodger claimed the pole for the Milwaukee 200. He led the first 59 laps before being overtaken by Bettenhausen. The Watson roadster wasn't running right and spun on lap 64. Rodger kept it rolling and returned to competition, but

Top left: Johnny Thomson (left) and Johnny White (right). Although Thomson recorded only seven national championship victories, for several years he was a threat to qualify up front and win every race. White's championship career lasted only 11 races, but he was a highly touted prospect to be a big star. Sprint cars bit both; Thomson was killed at Allentown, Pennsylvania, and White was left a quadriplegic from injuries at Terre Haute, Indiana. *Ken Coles*

Top right: At DuQuoin in 1960, Rodger has just told Watson that the engine has a miss. Rodger qualified 11th and dropped out after 34 laps with a handling problem. *Ken Coles*

Above: Rodger qualified on the pole and finished 14th after the magneto quit while leading on lap 69 in the 1960 Hoosier Hundred. *Ken Coles*

Above left: Roger McCluskey won the 1973 National Championship and became the president of USAC after he retired. *Ken Coles*

Above right: Rodger received the 1960 Sportsmanship Award from the Hoosier Auto Racing Fans (HARF). Gene Powlen presents the silver tray. *C. V. Haschel photo, Author Collection*

Right: Among the off-season banquets, HARF held one of the biggest for decades. In January 1961, Rodger was honored with HARF's Sportsmanship Award for the 1960 season. Back row, left to right: Russ Sweedler, Ray Duckworth, "Wild Willie" Wildhaber, Paul Hopper, Bob Wente, Charlie Mayer, Bud Bogard, Ronnie Duman. Front row, seated left to right: Bobby Grim, Leon Clum, Gene Powlen, Rodger, Tom Cherry, A. J. Foyt. *C. V. Haschel photo, Author Collection*

35 laps later, he was sidelined with an overheating problem. Len Sutton ran a steady race from 11th to win over Foyt, making it the third consecutive year the Oregonian visited victory lane.

At DuQuoin, Rodger dropped out, reporting a handling problem as A. J. Foyt won his first national championship event at the wheel of the Bowes Seal Fast Meskowski/Kuzma/Bignotti dirt car. Returning to Indianapolis as the defending champion of the Hoosier Hundred, Rodger again took the pole, breaking the track record in the process. But a magneto problem put

the Leader Card Duo on the trailer, having led the first 68 laps. With three events remaining, Foyt's victory put him within striking distance of Ward, who still led even though he hadn't added any points for six races.

Leading the now-hot championship battle to Trenton, Rodger qualified 14th and spent a busy day working to the front. He passed Foyt for the lead on lap 80, but four circuits later Sachs was by both of them and tallied his first win of the season. Ward's second place finish only delayed Foyt's march to the title.

Above: At Indianapolis in 1961, Rodger qualified fourth, led seven laps, and finished third. This was the only time that Watson tried coil springs on the roadsters he built. The idea came from watching the Cooper test at Indy. *Armin Krueger*

Left: Ready to qualify at the Speedway in 1961. Behind Del Webb's Sun City-sponsored car is Steve Stapp (third from right), who would become a highly successful sprint car owner and builder. Steve's father, Babe Stapp, competed in the championship series from 1927 until 1940. *Ken Coles*

Opposite top left: Ward visits with Jack Brabham and car owner John Cooper during practice for the 1961 Indy 500. He arranged a test session for Brabham and the Cooper-Climax at the Speedway, late in 1960. Rodger explained, "I drove the car at one point during practice, and said to John, 'That is the future—but you got to find some horsepower. . . .'" Brabham finished ninth and is credited with starting the rear-engine revolution. *Armin Krueger*

Opposite top right: Rodger is interviewed over the Speedway's public address after qualifying. *Ken Coles*

Left: In the garage area after qualifying, Rodger enjoys getting together with fans as much as they liked meeting an Indy winner. *Ken Coles*

Right: Along pit lane, Rodger and Bob Wilke talk business with Speedway owner Tony Hulman (facing the camera in his traditional suit and tie). *Ken Coles*

Rodger passing Troy Ruttman at Milwaukee. In an interview years later, Rodger spoke frankly about Ruttman, who was a midget champion while still a teenager and an Indy winner at age 22. Ruttman continued to be a hard racer into the mid-1960s. "I thought Ruttman was probably as great a race driver as we have ever known. He had a few problems mentally and didn't behave himself like he should have. When you beat him, though, you thought it was a miracle." *Armin Krueger*

Qualifying sixth at Sacramento, the Leader Card Offy burned a piston on the first lap and Rodger could only watch Foyt claim his third victory of the year and the point lead. The Bobby Ball Memorial at the Phoenix Fairgrounds wrapped up the title for the young Texan as Ward qualified 13th and didn't get any faster. After being lapped by Foyt, he spun out of the race on lap 83. Foyt had captured wins in four of the last six races, and after such a strong start to the season, Rodger finished 290 points behind the new champion in the final standings.

Rodger racing with Len Sutton in 1961. Ward started second and led all 100 laps at Milwaukee in June. That winter, Wilke and Watson would choose Sutton to be Ward's teammate. *Armin Krueger*

Rodger didn't do a lot of sprint car racing. Here he's battling with Parnelli Jones at Indianapolis Raceway Park. Jones won his second of three consecutive USAC sprint car titles in 1961. *Ken Coles*

1961

Rodger qualified fourth for his first race in the new Leader Card dirt car when the season opened at Trenton, but suffered an engine problem after 32 laps, running third. He was credited with an 18th place finish while Eddie Sachs earned the win. Rodger now had a teammate as Watson built a second car for Johnny Boyd.

When Indy opened, the collective attention focused on the first 150-mile-per-hour lap. It came as little surprise when Tony Bettenhausen appeared to take the head of the line in the Autolite Epperly, turning faster laps each day of practice and flirting with the high 149s. Then the Friday before pole qualifying, while waiting to make another late run, Tony agreed to test Paul Russo's Stearly Motor Freight Watson, the car that

At the wheel of the Leader Card sprint car at Indianapolis Raceway Park. Not only was Rodger an original invester in the facility, he was instrumental in the layout of its oval and road course. *Ken Coles*

A New Kind of Car

While at Sebring the year before, Rodger had suggested that Jack Brabham should test the Cooper at Indy to see how it adapted to the big oval. Brabham replied that he would give the idea some thought. In October, Rodger received a phone call from Jack, who was on his way to Watkins Glen and was interested in stopping at Indianapolis. Only too happy to phone Tony Hulman, Rodger quickly set up a testing session.

Rodger recalled, "He ran probably 40–50 laps. Then he said, 'Rodger, if you let me go in the other direction, I can go even faster.'" Ward jumped at an offer to take some laps in the car and found that although he could barely see over the windshield, the car was comfortable and quick. The result of this test was that John Cooper decided to build a new car for the next year's Indy 500, with the Coventry-Climax engine increased to 2.8 liters.

Ward had driven to victory in 1959. Russo was having difficulty finding speed and sought another opinion.

Tragically, after a couple of laps, the car veered sharply to the right on the front stretch and climbed the wall. Collecting the wire fencing above the wall, the car began barrel-rolling, knocking down posts and wrapping itself in cables and wire. Doctors said that Bettenhausen was dead before the car started to burn and even quick emergency work had no opportunity to save him. An investigation determined that the cause of the wreck was a bolt holding the front axle that worked free when the brakes were applied.

On Sunday, May 28, Foyt won the first race on a 5/8-mile dirt oval at Indianapolis Raceway Park in Clermont, a USAC sprint car event. Rodger had been involved with the design of both the oval and road course, specifying a three-tiered approach for banking the oval's turns and developing the initial layout for the road track. A month later, the oval was paved and Sachs won a stock car race.

With sponsorship from Del Webb's Sun City, Rodger was in a new Watson roadster that looked identical to its predecessors, but the 1961 design differed from the rest in that it employed coil springs instead of torsion bars. Calling them

Rodger qualified seventh but only lasted a dozen laps in the 1961 Hoosier Hundred. *Ken Coles*

Left: Rodger relaxes in the cockpit of his Watson roadster early in the 1962 season. Years later, he said, "When I look back at my career and think how lucky I was to do the things that I've done. . . How many people do you know who can truthfully say that they've fulfilled their lifetime's ambition? Not too many people. Well, you're sitting with one." *Ken Coles*

Right: With A. J. Watson and crew in 1962. Watson's pit crewmen were again the models of efficiency, as Rodger completed three pit stops in just 60 seconds. Curiously, Sutton's three stops also totaled 60 seconds. No one had faster stops during the Memorial Day classic. *Rodger Ward Jr.*

Left: The crew of Bobby Marshman's Bryant Heating & Cooling Epperly strip the chassis after qualifying. *Armin Krueger*

Right: John Posey, a photographer for *Floyd Clymer's Indy Yearbook*, reported a friendly rivalry between the crews of Ward and Sutton in 1962. He called the Leader Card team "probably the greatest racing organization ever put together." *IMS Photo*

Left: Chickie Hirashima, crew chief for Len Sutton's team, upgrades the signage above the Leader Card garages. Hirashima had been at the Speedway since the mid-1930s when he was a riding mechanic with Rex Mays. In his book, *My Road to Indy,* Sutton admits that people frequently ask whether Wilke and Watson had told him not to challenge Rodger for the win. "The fact is that Chickie would have given me the world if I would have passed Ward and won the race. There was definitely no deal before or during the race as to our positions. The one thing I am sure of, neither one of us would have risked taking the other out trying to get to the finish line first." *Steve Zautke Collection*

Right: Parnelli Jones figured out his own way to drive Indy and it was fast. In 1962, he fulfilled all expectations when he was the first, and the only, driver to qualify faster than 150 miles per hour. Car owner J. C. Agajanian relishes the celebration. *Ken Coles*

"terrible cars" Watson later admitted this was the biggest mistake he made in his roadster chassis development and the coils were gone the next year. Still, Rodger qualified fourth at Indianapolis and ran up front all day, leading seven laps. As Eddie Sachs and A. J. Foyt fought for the win, Ward was out of touch in third. In another dramatic finish, Foyt didn't receive any fuel on his last stop when the nozzle malfunctioned. Forced to make another stop while leading with less than 20 laps to go, Foyt thought he and his team had given the race away. But Sachs pitted just three laps from the checkers when the cord began to show through his right rear tire, and Foyt made his first trip to Indy's Victory Lane.

Quietly, but not unnoticed, Jack Brabham put the Cooper Climax solidly into the race. While out-muscled on the straightaways, the car was also at a distinct disadvantage when it caught a roadster in a turn. With the roadster filling the groove, Brabham wasn't able to take advantage of its agility and then had to watch the roadster pull away again on the straightaway. Yet with a ninth place run, it proved its durability and the Aussie made a lot of friends.

The new Watson was the class of the field when the tour convened for Milwaukee's 100-lap event, just five days later. Ward qualified outside of Dick Rathmann on the front row and led into the first turn. That was the closest anyone else came

Left: Rodger was just a couple of ticks behind Parnelli with his 149.3 average, earning the middle of the front row, the best starting spot of his career. *Armin Krueger*

Below: Parnelli is ready to head onto the track for his record-breaking 150-mile-per-hour qualifying run. *Ken Coles*

A. J. Foyt is ready to qualify. He would time fifth quickest and start immediately behind Rodger. The defending race winner, Foyt led laps 60 and 61 before heading to the pits. When the car stalled and wouldn't re-fire, the crew began pushing it back to the garage. But when Foyt let out the clutch while it was being wheeled away, the engine surprisingly fired and he quickly rejoined the race. Unfortunately, a wheel that had been left loose came off in a turn and Foyt spun into the infield, ending his day. *Ken Coles*

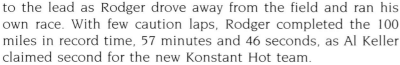

to the lead as Rodger drove away from the field and ran his own race. With few caution laps, Rodger completed the 100 miles in record time, 57 minutes and 46 seconds, as Al Keller claimed second for the new Konstant Hot team.

A magneto failure put Rodger out of Milwaukee's Fair Week 200-miler in August, after he started third and led 17 laps. At Springfield, the day before Milwaukee, he had burned a piston in practice. However, it rained before the race started and the makeup date was the day after Milwaukee. Teams packed in the rain, drove 300 miles from Springfield to Milwaukee, and then ran the 200-mile race on the pavement. Then they loaded up again and retraced their tracks to Springfield in time to race the next day. With Watson needing to change the engine in the Leader Card dirt car, Rodger was available to drive the Dean Van Lines Kuzma at Springfield, giving Sachs who had taken a hard hit at Milwaukee a rest. After starting in the last row, his sixth place finish added 80 more points in the standings.

With just a handful of races left in the season, Rodger turned the fastest qualifying lap at Syracuse. Repeating his performance at Milwaukee in June, he led every lap and his 95-mile-per-hour 100-lap average set a new record for that track. In Indianapolis' Hoosier Hundred, Rodger had to get out of the groove to avoid a spinning Hurtubise. When he dropped out after just a dozen laps, he was mathematically eliminated from winning the championship. A week later at Trenton, in the last race before heading west, Ward finished third in the roadster behind the dirt cars of Sachs and Hurtubise.

Rodger qualified second for the annual race at Sacramento's fairgrounds and took the early lead from new record holder Shorty Templeman. Foyt worked past Rodger on lap 28 as the track became more difficult with ruts and blowing dust. Then he burned a piston on the 75th circuit, thus returning Rodger to the lead. The conditions were so treacherous that A. J. complained to the officials, recommending that they stop the race early. Running behind Ward, Roger McCluskey's engine stalled when his car bounced roughly on the 82nd lap. Calling on all 15 years of experience, Rodger avoided trouble and the Leader Card team had a hard-earned third victory of the year.

The season closed at Phoenix, where Rodger captured his fourth front-row start of the year, outside of another new record holder, pole-sitter Al Keller. Rodger was able to grab the lead from Keller before they completed the first lap. While Ward worked hard to keep Parnelli Jones behind him, Keller fell back while trying to come to grips with a surface that was turning into a replay of Sacramento. On the leader's 42nd lap, Keller hit a rut in the fourth turn, jerking the car sideways. It snap-rolled, then cartwheeled into the infield. Keller, who was having his best year, couldn't be revived when medical help reached him.

Jones passed Ward when the race restarted, but after three laps it was stopped short of halfway in order to allow track workers to attempt to repair the surface so the race could be completed. Jones spun on the subsequent restart and Rodger retook the point, but Parnelli kept his car going and fought back to retake the lead 15 laps later. When Chuck Hulse flipped five times on the 89th circuit and escaped without serious injury, the race was stopped for good and Parnelli Jones had his first championship victory.

Rodger enjoys the spoils of Victory Lane for the second time at Indianapolis in 1962. Only five drivers before him (Milton, Meyers, Shaw, Rose, and Vukovich) had won Indy more than once. IMS Photo

Rodger's second place finish gave him two wins, a second, and a third in the season's last five races, with only the third place at Trenton being on the pavement. While Foyt claimed his second national title, Rodger came home third, trailing Sachs by 80 points.

In November, Rodger joined a team of drivers from USAC (Len Sutton and Paul Goldsmith) and NASCAR (Marvin Panch, Fireball Roberts, and Joe Weatherly) for a unique endurance test featuring two street Pontiacs prepared by ace mechanic Ray Nichels. Making 24-hour runs, first at Indianapolis and then another at Darlington, the six traded off driving 1–1 1/2-hour shifts, changing when they stopped for tires or fuel. The runs established new 24-hour records, averaging 107 and 108 miles per hour, with the fastest speed being 108.8 miles per hour at Darlington.

1962

When Wilke and Watson decided to continue the two-car team for the new season, they hired Len Sutton for the second car. With 50 national championship starts and three victories in the seven previous seasons, Sutton was highly respected. In preparation for the season, Watson built a new car for Ward and switched the coil springs from the 1961 cars to his preferred four-bar suspension. On the home front, Rodger and Jo had separated over the winter, and Jo was filing divorce papers. Rodger had moved within walking distance of the Speedway, and Rodger Jr. and his younger brother, David, frequently stayed at the apartment.

The national championship season opened at Trenton and Rodger qualified his 1961 roadster fourth, giving him the best seat in the house for the battle between Foyt and Jones. He finished third, while Foyt scrambled past Jones on the 27th lap and claimed the first trophy of the year.

When Indy opened, a very obvious improvement brought increased speed and safety. All the front-stretch bricks had been paved over, with the exception of a yard-wide strip across the track at the finish line. Although Brabham and Cooper hadn't returned, California's Mickey Thompson brought a pair of cars of his own design—with the Buick engine behind the driver—

and offered one of the seats to rookie Dan Gurney. Thompson had frequently been in the headlines with his attempts to break the land speed record at Bonneville. A third Thompson-built car was entered by Jim Kimberly.

Parnelli Jones hogged the headlines as he began knocking on the door of a 150-mile-per-hour lap early in the month, again at the wheel of Agajanian's three-year old Watson. Several stopwatches caught Jones with a 151-mile-per-hour lap at one

point. Bobby Marshman was right behind him in the year-old Bryant Heating and Cooling Epperly, turning 149-plus circuits with seeming ease. When it came time to run for the pole, Sutton was the second car to take the green and set the bar high with record-breaking laps that averaged 149.328. But it was Jones who claimed the 150 silver dollars, with each of his four laps run in less than a minute and an average of 150.370. Marshman later timed at 149.347, but Rodger's 149.371 earned

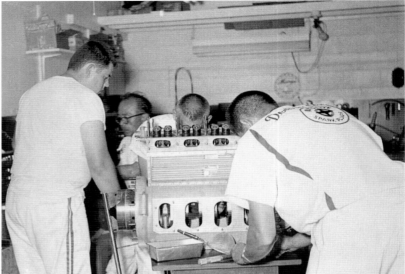

Above: The year of 1963 was the last hurrah for the roadsters, before they made room at the top for the rear engine cars. Rodger qualified and finished fourth at Indianapolis behind Jones, Formula 1 star Jimmy Clark, and Foyt. *Ken Coles*

Top left: Tonawanda, New York's Jim Hurtubise was a tenacious competitor, whether in sprint, stock, or champ cars. He scored all four of his national tour wins in his first four seasons, the last being at the Illinois State Fairgrounds in Springfield in 1962. *Ken Coles*

Top right: While A. J. Watson is usually credited with the success of his roadsters, many would be surprised to learn that he also did all of his own engine work. Here, he's working on an Offy in Gasoline Alley during May. *Ken Coles*

the center seat in the front row and moved Marshman outside and Sutton back to fourth.

At age 41, Rodger's 11 consecutive starts at Indy were tops among active drivers, as were his 16 championship wins and cumulative 9,696 series points. Many picked Ward and Sutton as favorites to win. Confident he had a fast car and could race with Parnelli later, and that Watson and his crew would keep him near the front, Rodger watched Parnelli drive into the lead and settled into third behind Foyt.

Foyt pitted on lap 69 with a brake problem and Rodger took second. The Bowes car had difficulty restarting and then lost a wheel when Foyt returned to the track, taking him out of the race. A few laps later, Jones drove through the pits, yelling something about his brakes to crew chief Johnny Pouelsen. Running laps at over 146 miles per hour, Ward closed the gap to Jones but fell back to fifth when he pitted. Quickly passing Don Davis, Eddie Sachs, and Troy Ruttman, he was second when Jones headed to the pits. As Rodger hurried into the lead, Parnelli dragged a crewman the length of three pits before the car stopped.

With Jones dropping well back, only his teammate would pose a threat and Len took the lead when Rodger pitted on lap 161. When Sutton pitted after nine laps out front, Rodger reclaimed the top spot. He ran the closing laps consistently, holding an 11-second lead over Sutton as he took the checkered flag. With third-place Sachs 20 seconds behind, it was the closest 1-2-3 finish since 1911. Completing the 500 miles in just under 3 hours and 34 minutes, Rodger averaged 140.293 miles per hour, faster than the previous record by more than one full mile per hour.

The Lotus-Fords showed how effective they were on tracks shorter than Indianapolis' 2.5 miles when Colin Chapman and Jimmy Clark took them to Milwaukee. Clark set new records for his qualifying lap and for the 200-mile race as he led every lap. Rodger finished fourth. *Armin Krueger*

While Rodger raced his Cooper-Monaco at Mosport, Canada, the next Saturday, Sutton practiced with both cars for the Milwaukee 100. Although Sutton was slightly quicker in Ward's car, when Rodger returned on Sunday, he didn't qualify fast enough to make the field. After changes, he won the consolation race and started the 100-mile race last. Turning the day around, Rodger drove to a fourth place finish as Foyt earned the win. Unfortunately, Sutton was hospitalized with crushed vertebrae and a collapsed lung when a brake cylinder failed and he slammed the wall viciously while running second.

Celebration

Later, after the Indy 500 victory ceremonies, photographs, and interviews, Rodger picked up Rodger Jr. and David and headed downtown. Rodger Jr. recalls, "Someplace in Indianapolis, I couldn't find it now, there were the gentleman's barbershops. My dad, David, and I went downtown and we went to one of those basement barbershops, off of Capitol or Meridian. We got haircuts, facials, manicures, shoe shines, and the whole works."

Rodger is racing with Johnny Boyd and Len Sutton. Boyd was his Leader Card teammate in 1961 and Sutton in 1962 (until his accident at Milwaukee) and for several races in 1963. *Armin Krueger*

Rodger returned to Mosport with the Nichels Engineering Pontiac team and collected a win in the USAC stock car race on June 23rd. While Nichels' driver, Paul Goldsmith, won 10 races and earned his second stock car title, Rodger and Nichels drivers A. J. Foyt and Len Sutton all finished top 10 in points.

Starting on the front row outside of Foyt, Rodger earned a rain-shortened victory at Trenton in July and held a 600-point lead over Parnelli and Don Davis. Then Rodger drove the Leader Card midget in the Hoosier Grand Prix on the Indianapolis Raceway Park road course. Jim Hall was declared the overall winner after he finished third in the first heat, following Roger Penske and Gurney; then Jim ran second to Hap Sharp in the second heat. Ward's fifth and third place finishes earned second in the overall standings.

When the tour returned to Milwaukee for the 200-mile event, Rodger was pressed hard by Foyt, but extended to six his run of consecutive years with visits to Milwaukee's victory lane. Foyt—who had left Bignotti and the Bowes car after Trenton and was in his second race with Lindsey Hopkins and crew chief Jack Beckley—used all of his tricks trying to get past Ward. But for nearly 60 laps, Rodger was unmoved.

Skipping Langhorne where Don Branson claimed his first championship win while taking Sutton's place with Leader Card, Rodger collected the Syracuse 100-miler two weeks later. He started and finished fifth in the Hoosier Hundred, then led at Trenton until brushing the wall and spinning at lap 132. Rodger

Them's the Brakes

Three weeks after Trenton, in 1962, Rodger was driving a sports car built by Frank Coons and Jim Travers (who he still called "the rich kids") before the Los Angeles Times Grand Prix at Riverside.

"That S.O.B., you could light the tires in third gear if you really got after it strong. I was excited as hell," Rodger said, explaining how his season ended. "I was warming the car up and trying to get the feel. I really cranked it on going up through the esses, came around down the back straightaway, and got to turn nine and everything was fine. I came around to turn one and was in third gear, I think, and running probably 120 miles per hour and got off the throttle and hit the brakes so I could make the turn, and I didn't have any brakes. I knew that trying to make the turn was useless, so I just decided to go straight ahead. I went off a rather large embankment and landed on the pavement where a road came under the racetrack through a tunnel, and then went through another fence. I'm laying in the hospital and I'm thinking to myself that was a hell of a fall." After spending nearly a week in the hospital, Rodger was released clad in a cast from the waist up.

was push-started and registered another fifth place finish, while Branson scored his second win in the Leader Card dirt car and Sutton finished second in his return from injuries. With Jud Phillips now the crew chief of the second team, Watson—as the team manager and car builder—had six victories in the season's first 11 races, including three on pavement miles, two on dirt, and the win at Indy. Fortunately, the fifth place finish at Trenton locked up the championship.

1963

While Watson was busy building eight new roadsters, two for Leader Card and an unprecedented six customer orders during the off-season, Colin Chapman's Lotus factory was fabricating two new cars specifically for Indianapolis. Chapman not only had new Ford engines on the way, but he also had Ford funding for his program and Dan Gurney and Jimmy Clark for drivers.

Joining Bill Stroppe's three-car Mercury team for the Daytona 500, Rodger made it as far as nine laps into the 250-mile qualifier before his engine let go. His teammates, Parnelli Jones and Darel Dieringer, finished eighth and ninth, while a young Texan named Johnny Rutherford took the win in Smoky Yunick's Chevy. A second race for Stroppe came at Atlanta in March, with Troy Ruttman in a fourth car. This time Rodger

completed 242 laps before the Mercury's engine gave up, and he was rewarded with $325 for 27th position.

Rodger was ready to race when the season opened at Trenton. But after qualifying sixth in his dirt car, he was sidelined with a fuel leak at 43 laps. He and his team headed home to get ready for Indy.

With sponsorship from Kaiser Aluminum, Rodger qualified his new roadster fourth for the 500, with one lap over 150 miles per hour and the average just under that milestone. Parnelli topped 151 and would again start from the pole. Jim Hurtubise put the Novi second—with Don Branson on his outside—at the wheel of the third Leader Card entry, the roadster Rodger had driven to victory the year before. Next to Rodger in the middle of the second row was Clark, who was considered a rookie, in the new Lotus.

While Hurtubise shoved the supercharged V-8 Novi to the front for the first lap, Jones took over on the second and opened a comfortable lead, turning laps in the 150-mile-per-hour range. For most of the early going, the Novi kept a strong pack of cars bottled up behind it, and Ward found himself dicing with that group as each driver waited for the chance to get past. But by lap 40, he had slipped back to 10th. Hurtubise's Novi dropped out of the race just past halfway with an oil leak, having run

In 1963, Rodger put the Kaiser Aluminum Watson dirt car on the pole for the Hoosier Hundred and led every lap. He set new qualifying and 100-lap race records as he claimed his third win of the season.
Ken Coles

For three years, from 1962 through 1964, Bobby Marshman was one of the fastest racers on the championship trail. *Ken Coles*

lead on lap 68 and holding it to the finish for his seventh win on the Milwaukee oval. He earned his third victory of the year at Springfield in August, passing Foyt on the 63rd circuit.

After a successful testing session at Milwaukee, Clark and Gurney joined the championship series for their first race outside of Indianapolis in Milwaukee's annual 200-miler. The Lotus-Fords qualified first and second, with Clark's time easily breaking the track record. The Scotsman led flag to flag and broke the record for the fastest 200-mile race, averaging 104.4 miles per hour. Starting 14th, Rodger's Kaiser Aluminum roadster finished fourth on the same lap as Gurney, and he moved to second in the points trailing Foyt.

Although Rodger was the senior driver on the circuit, he wasn't ready to slow down. Heading to DuQuoin Fairground mile, he claimed the pole with a record 105.3-mile-per-hour lap and charged into the lead at the start. The only one who could catch him was Foyt, and on the 43rd lap he passed Rodger and drove away. When Rodger finished second a half-circuit behind, he was the only car still on the same lap as Foyt. The Texan now owned a 590-point lead over Ward and the next stop was the Hoosier Hundred, the richest dirt car race on the championship schedule.

At the Indiana State Fairgrounds, Rodger improved on his DuQuoin performance. Again he broke the one-lap record, raising it to 93.5 miles per hour, and jumped into the lead at the green flag. This time no one caught him as he led Branson to the checkers by 13 seconds. Foyt outdueled another young Texan, Johnny Rutherford, for third, keeping a strong hold on the point lead with only three races remaining. The next day, Parnelli beat Rodger in USAC's stock car 250 at Milwaukee; they were both driving Mercurys.

When Rodger's roadster developed a fuel leak after only six laps at Trenton, he was mathematically eliminated from the

in the top five until encountering problems. By the three-quarter mark, Rodger was up to seventh with the two Lotuses, plus Foyt and McCluskey, ahead of him all chasing Jones.

No one could catch Parnelli, although Clark tried to close the gap in his Lotus. Then the drama of the race came when *Calhoun* (the name Jones had given to his car) began trailing smoke. With evidence of oil building along the tail of Jones's roadster, USAC's Harlan Fengler was close to ordering the black flag for the leader. But making a very conspicuous argument along the main straightaway, J. C. Agajanian convinced Fengler that the smoke was from oil being blown onto the header and the leak had already stopped. Fifteen minutes later, Parnelli took the checkered flag and when McCluskey spun out on the last lap, Rodger claimed fourth finishing position.

Rodger started the Leader Card roadster third at Milwaukee. Hurtubise led early but spun in turn two and was passed by Foyt. Rodger chased Foyt for the next 22 circuits, taking the

Pushers

By mid-summer 1963, Watson had put out the word that he wasn't going to build any more roadsters. Ward reportedly had said he wanted a rear-engine car for 1964. Watson had never built a "pusher," but that was a small detail. He had the rest of the summer to figure it out.

Left: The *Ray Mann Spl.* was also known as the *Burnett-Chevy*. Mann first became involved in racing as a photographer in the Pacific Northwest. About 1950, he tried his hand at racing midgets with mixed success. He moved to Indianapolis in the late 1950s and founded *Racing Pictorial* magazine, which was first published in 1959. He also became a partner with Rodger and A. J. Watson in Ward and Watson Service, a Mobil gas station which had been owned by Mike Petrovich. Eventually, both Ward and Mann were among the original stockholders in Indianapolis Raceway Park. *C. V. Haschel photo, Author Collection*

Below: Rodger set a new one-lap record at DuQuoin in 1963, and led the first 42 laps of the race. Foyt (2) caught him and won the race with Rodger in second. Ward trailed Foyt in the final standings by more than 700 points. *Gene Crucean Collection*

small glimmer of hope he still held for the championship. Of even greater significance was the performance by Clark and Gurney in the Lotuses, who topped qualifying and dominated much of the race in their first visit to the New Jersey oval. A weakness in the Lotus became apparent, however, when Clark dropped out after 49 laps and Gurney did the same nearly 100 laps later, both while leading and from the same ailment—a broken oil line. This gave the victory to Foyt, who had lapped the field in his roadster.

For the first time since 1948, the championship trail headed west without going through Syracuse, New York, there being a conflict with available race dates and a revised state fair schedule. The track wouldn't return to the national schedule and Rodger was the winner of its last two championship events.

He also won the final two events of the year. When he took the checkered flag at Sacramento after capturing the pole and leading 88 laps, he joined Jimmy Bryan as the only three-time winners on that fairground oval. The Phoenix win was a little tougher, as he qualified for the ninth starting spot. But among the lessons he had learned in his years on the dirt tracks was that it was a lot easier to catch and pass cars when they were running close together, and he passed three cars on the first lap and another three on the second. On the sixth lap he grabbed second from Rutherford, and on the 31st he overtook Chuck Hulse for the lead and then put some ground between them. His fifth victory of the year was the most wins he had scored in any season of the championship.

Left: Rodger had enough points to secure his second national championship when he was injured at Riverside late in 1962. Here, he receives the trophy for the championship. *Rodger Ward Jr.*

Opposite top left: Rodger Ward Jr. recalls the time when his father showed him his personal pocket calendar. "Right after the '62 win—he was very image conscious—my dad always had the very nice thin black calendar. One time he said to me, 'You know, I never let anybody look in my book. I want to show you something.' He pulls it out and there on May 30th it simply says, 'Win The Race!'" *Steve Zautke*

Oppisite top right: Rodger and Bob Wilke relax between qualifying and the race at Milwaukee. While Wilke ran Leader Cards, a Milwaukee-based producer of commercial paper products, he had been active in midget racing since the late 1930s. He was the epitome of the era's car owners. In the 1950s and 1960s, before the days of sponsor-financed racing, they could scarcely look at competing on the circuit as a business. J. C. Agajanian once explained, "After you get past the first three places, the purses aren't big enough to cover expenses. I had a pretty good year last year and lost $34,000." (From "The Owner Makes The Profit—Rarely!" by Jerrold Footlick, *1962 Clymer Yearbook) Steve Zautke*

Opposite bottom left: A. J. Watson admitted that when he learned Bob Wilke had hired Rodger, he probably didn't think Rodger had what it took to win Indy. "I thought it was all right. He was the best cut that was available at the time so we went for it. And it worked out. He drove for me for seven years and he has probably put me on Broadway more than anybody else. I mean, we won a lot of races. He went fast and was easy to get along with. It just worked out." *Steve Zautke*

Watkins Glen

In spite of his painful wreck at Riverside, Rodger had developed a fondness for road racing and purchased a Cooper-Monaco. Late in the year, he ran second to Lloyd Ruby in a road race at Kent, Washington. His next stop was the U.S. Grand Prix being competed at Watkins Glen. In his second effort for that race, Rodger qualified 17th in a year-old Reg Parnell Racing Lotus 24 powered by a V-8 BRM engine, and his race lasted 44 laps before he retired with a gearbox failure.

Above: Mechanic Tiny Worley confers with Rodger about his Nichels Engineering Pontiac at Indianapolis Raceway Park in 1961. Rodger collected five USAC stock car victories during his career, including one with Nichels' team in Mosport, Canada, in June 1962. *Wayne Bryant photo, Ted Knorr Collection*

#17 ROGER WARD - 1964 USAC MERCURY MARAUDER

Rodger is ready for work in his Bill Stroppe Mercury. With the backing of the Ford Motor Company, Stroppe prepared one of the top stock car racing teams in the early 1960s, competing in both USAC and National Association for Stock Car Racing (NASCAR). Ward won at Milwaukee and Ascot in this car. *Author Collection*

Chapter 6

Rear Engine Cars

Although he had been bumped at Indy, Len Sutton ran four races with Leader Card in 1963. Back in his home in Portland, Oregon, Rolla Vollstedt—who had fielded cars for Sutton throughout his career, including roadsters, sprinters, and big cars—began building a rear-engine Indianapolis car in his basement, working with designers Don Robison and John Feuz. Len arranged for them to take the completed Vollstedt to a Goodyear tire test at Indianapolis that fall, where he turned laps over 153 miles per hour, fastest of all of the cars at the test. This caught A. J. Watson's attention and he built two cars based on the Vollstedt design. In March of 1964, with Grant King now helping out, Sutton tested at Indy again and once again turned the fastest lap at 154.9.

Right: Rodger Ward Jr. and his father at the Speedway in 1964. An Army medic, Rodger Jr. was shipping out for Turkey the next day. *Rodger Ward Jr.*

Opposite: By 1964, the battle between the two tire giants, Firestone and Goodyear, was just heating up. Rodger tested for both companies; here he and Watson are working on a Firestone test. *Photo courtesy of the Indianapolis Motor Speedway*

1964

Rodger got his racing started in January, rejoining Stroppe's stock car team with Jones and Dieringer and additions Dave MacDonald and Chuck Daigh, for Riverside's Motor Trend 500. But it was another early exit when the transmission on his Mercury failed after 24 circuits. Dan Gurney claimed the victory.

When the national championship season opened in March, it was at the paved oval just constructed west of Phoenix. While Foyt led the inauguration, Rodger started and finished fifth in his 1963 roadster. Next up was Trenton where Rodger would debut Watson's rear-engine car.

Although Watson's machine resembled Sutton's Vollstedt, there was a major difference: while Vollstedt had an Offy, Watson received one of Ford's new DOHC V-8s, which was also making its first appearance. Rodger was off to a great start when he put the Watson outside of Foyt on the front row, just a tick slower than Foyt's record qualifying lap. Although he outran Foyt to the first turn, Foyt beat him to the third and took the lead. On the 38th lap, two slower cars running in a bigger pack got together in turn three just as Rodger was trying to follow Foyt past. Ed Kostenuk and Mario Andretti, who was making

50 cents

"I was about 16 years old working at Herb and Chuck's Service Station on Pico near Redondo Boulevard in L.A. in the late '40s. I had lived in that area all my life and somehow got a job there pumping gas. It was a big station for the time, having about eight gas pumps in front and a long building across the back with about six bays for offices, body shop, paint shop, and whatever.

"I wanted to work there because Bud Murphy kept his midget there and it was like heaven for me to be near a race car. My friend and fellow race fan, Phil Seeberg, also worked there. Johnny Mantz and Rodger were both driving the Murphy midget off and on, and would just hang around sometimes.

"One day, Phil and I were standing in front of the office and here comes Rodger in a brand new, big, black Caddie convertible with the top down, of course. He has a beautiful blond in the front seat next to him and stops the car right in front of us. Rodger gets out and walks over to us and sheepishly asks to borrow gas money! Phil loans him 50 cents, and off he goes. We saw him many times after that but we never brought it up and he never did pay Phil back!

"The last time I talked to Rodger was about eight years ago at the NHRA Museum during one of the California Racer Reunions. He was getting very old then, but he did remember those days at Herb and Chuck's. I never brought up the fifty cents."

Roy C. Morris, San Juan Capistrano, California

his first championship start, both spun and Rodger was unable to avoid Kostenuk's machine. The damaged front suspension gave Watson some extra work before Indianapolis opened.

On a trip to Daytona in 1963, Rodger had met Diane Blauvelt, who caught his eye while singing in a lounge Rodger visited. After a brief courtship, Rodger brought her back to Indianapolis, where they were married. Diane was pregnant with their first child during the winter and on May 17, Sunday of the first qualifying weekend at Indianapolis, she presented him with a son. They named him Richard.

Rodger was quickly over 150 miles per hour on his first day of practice for the 500, but that would hardly make the race. Bobby Marshman's 158.7 was the month's fastest practice speed, but it was Jimmy Clark who claimed the pole with his best laps of the month, a 158.828-mile-per-hour average with his fastest circuit clocked at 159.337. Marshman was second best and Rodger qualified on the outside of the front row for the third time in his career. While the front row was all rear-engine machines, Parnelli and Foyt elected to run one more race in their roadsters and lined up fourth and fifth, with Gurney's Lotus sixth.

While Clark grabbed the lead on the opening lap, tragedy was unfolding behind him. As the leaders completed their second lap, the Mickey Thompson Sears Allstate machine of rookie Dave MacDonald lost control exiting turn four and slammed into the inside wall, becoming a fireball that ricocheted onto the track where it collected several other cars, including Eddie Sachs. Both Sachs' and MacDonald were killed and those out of the race included Johnny Rutherford and Bobby Unser.

Len Sutton, who was driving the car immediately behind MacDonald, wrote that MacDonald had passed him going into

A. J. Watson jump-started his rear-engine car-building process by borrowing his initial plan from Rolla Vollstedt's promising design and modifying it to suit his preferences. It was the first and probably the most successful of Watson's rear-engine race cars. *IMS Photo*

turn three and then looked inside of Walt Hansgen as they went into the fourth turn. When Hansgen took his normal line through the turn, MacDonald had to turn harder left to give him room and the back end of the little car quickly spun around. Sutton and Dick Rathmann made it past, but Sachs was right behind them (*My Road to Indy*; Sutton).

It took more than an hour and a half before the track was cleared and the race restarted. Clark's lead lasted until lap seven, when he was caught by Bobby Marshman. Running laps as high as 157 miles per hour, but using a little more than all of the apron in the turns, Marshman knocked the oil plug off his Lotus and was out of the race before the 40th lap. Clark led just eight more laps before his left rear suspension collapsed. Parnelli took the lead, but on his first pit stop a spark from the fuel filler cap blew the assembly off the tank of the car and it began to burn. Although he had started down pit lane, Jones quickly bailed out of the car as it rolled to a stop against the pit wall. At 55 laps, Foyt was the lead and Rodger was running second.

Rodger Jr. recalls the optimism the team had once the race got restarted. "At the start of the race, Rodg goes down in the corner in turn one, and both Foyt and Parnelli zoomed past him. Then they came off of two and Rodger picked up the throttle; he had to get all of the way out of the throttle and tap the brakes to keep from running into the both of them. He was that much faster than they were. The fact is that at lap 120, I polished my shoes."

Rodger ran a strong race, but the Ford V-8 was going through fuel much faster than expected. Foyt was uncontested in the last half of the race as Rodger made five pit stops to A. J.'s three, and trailed by 85 seconds at the checkers.

Climbing from the car, it quickly became apparent what had happened. Both Ward and Watson had wanted to run alcohol, while the other Ford-powered cars were using gasoline. Even though Ford's engine people had thwarted their attempts to practice with alcohol in the car, the decision was made on carburetion day to switch over before the race. The morning of the race, Watson explained that since they hadn't been able to practice with alcohol, he had installed a three-position control for Rodger to adjust the fuel mixture during the race.

The wreck that took the lives of Eddie Sachs and Dave MacDonald was one of the most vicious in Speedway history. Ronnie Duman's Trevis roadster exploded when the fuel tank ruptured and was virtually destroyed. Duman was able to escape with minor burns. *Steve Zautke*

Foyt chasing Ward during 1964's Indy 500. Foyt won his second and Rodger was the bridesmaid, but Rodger believed he would have won if he hadn't made a mistake with the fuel control valve mounted in the car. Lloyd Ruby and Johnny White were third and fourth, respectively. While the top teams were looking seriously at rear engine cars, the top four finishers were all in Watson-built machinery. But only Ward was not in a roadster. *IMS Photo*

"Since race drivers aren't all space scientists, I wanted to be damn sure I didn't make a mistake, so I wrote on the instrument panel 'forward—lean,'" Rodger later recalled. Then, he pointed out that the way the control was mounted on the right side of the cockpit, the lever could cut off the circulation to his leg when it was in the center position. A. J. went to work and turned the control so that it wouldn't rub against Rodger's leg and later explained the change to him.

As the race developed and they began to see the fuel being consumed at a rapid rate, Watson signaled Ward to *run lean.* But with the way the lever had been changed before the race, Rodger's moving it forward richened the mixture rather than making it lean.

For the rest of his life, Rodger thought he had the car capable of beating Foyt that day. "I could have won the race by half an hour; I could have won the race with four pit stops," he lamented. Then he added that Foyt had won it fair and square, noting, "I was the dumbshit that couldn't figure out which was lean or rich."

Above: Passing Troy Ruttman in the Dayton Steel Wheel Watson. For most of those who were at the Speedway that day, once the race restarted, it was shadowed by a big, dark cloud. *Armin Krueger*

Opposite above: Driving a Lotus 34, Parnelli Jones is leading Rodger in the Milwaukee 200. They finished first and second, and Jones's victory broke Foyt's string of seven straight wins. Foyt won all but three national championship events and dominated the 1964 season. For the second consecutive year, Rodger finished second to Foyt in the final standings. *Armin Krueger photo, Gene Crucean Collection*

Opposite below: Rodger signals to Foyt at Milwaukee in June. Ward qualified on the pole and took the lead from A. J. on lap 30. Twenty-three circuits later, Rodger was sidelined when the rear end packed up. *Ken Coles*

In the long run, Rodger also thought the second lap accident had a bearing on his handling of the race. "I was way out in front of them, but when I came around and saw that damned mess, I lost damn near any bit of enthusiasm I had for that

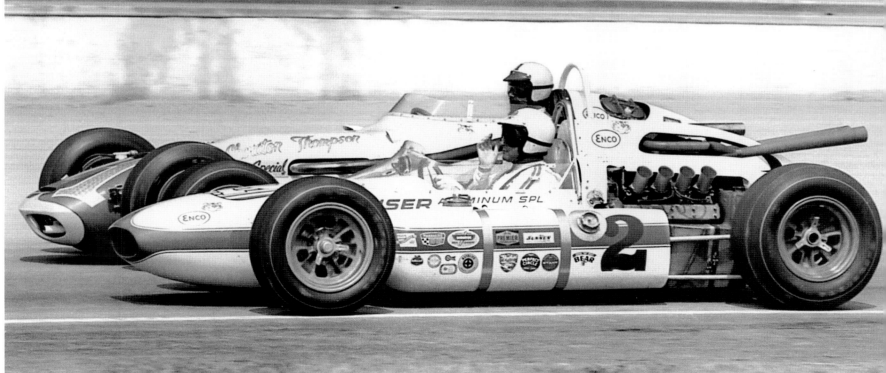

Rodger qualified fourth for the 1964 Hoosier Hundred and finished second to Foyt. No one realized it at the time, but this would be his last time to compete in the Hoosier Hundred and he would only run one more championship race on dirt. *Ken Coles*

race. It certainly didn't help my thinking. Then we sat there while they cleaned up the mess."

At Milwaukee, Foyt won again, partaking in his fourth consecutive victory lane ceremony. Rodger put the Watson-Ford on the pole and led 23 laps before the rear end failed. In fact, Foyt was on an unprecedented roll and won the first seven races before a transmission failure broke the streak in the Milwaukee 200, where Parnelli got the win. Foyt scored a total of 10 victories, his only other losses coming from mechanical failures— a clutch at Trenton and a blown engine that triggered a spin during the season's final event at Phoenix, won by Lloyd Ruby.

Among the toys Rodger had acquired was a personal airplane, and on August 19 he made the news when he had to land the plane on Interstate 74 after it developed engine trouble. He

still made it to Milwaukee for the USAC stock car race the next day. Teamed with Parnelli Jones in Bill Stroppe's Mercurys, Rodger handed his car over to Jones after Parnelli's dropped out early, and they shared victory lane.

It was the first season since 1956 that Rodger had gone without a win on the championship trail. Counting Indianapolis, he finished second four times, including Milwaukee, the Hoosier Hundred, and Phoenix. This netted second in the point standings, a distant 772 behind Foyt.

1965

Watson reworked his rear-engine design for the 1965 season, making major modifications. As had been his routine, he brought one of the 1964 cars to Phoenix for Rodger to drive in the opening round. Rodger qualified on the outside of the front row and led 50 laps, in spite of a spin to miss Rutherford's spinning car. But an engine failure while he was leading handed the victory to Don Branson, his teammate at the wheel of a roadster. The first dance for the new Watson was Trenton, where Rodger qualified third. Unfortunately, he was an early exit with a clutch failure after just 15 laps.

There was a lot to track when the Speedway opened on May 1. Foyt and Jones were in the Lotus 34s that had won on the trail during 1964. Gurney's All American Racers team was fielding his new Lotus. Mario Andretti was at the top of a bumper crop of rookies, with veteran mechanic Clint Brawner and a new rear-engine machine based on the design of Jack Brabham's 1964 Grand Prix car. McCluskey and another rookie, Joe Leonard, were in Shrikes built by Ted Halibrand and fielded by AAR. Colin Chapman was bringing the latest Lotus design— the 38—for Clark and Bobby Johns, another rookie. There were new British manufacturers contributing Lolas and BRPs. As expected, several well-used Watson, Kuzma, and Kurtis roadsters showed up. And for the second year in a row, Diane was expecting a baby in the middle of May.

While all of this was keeping the racing fans and news reporters busy, Watson and Ward were struggling through the worst month of May either had ever faced. The new *Moog St. Louis* Watson was proving to be a handful on the track. Also working against Rodger and A. J. were electrical and engine problems, including fried bearings and burned pistons.

Rodger Jr. remembered that the first day they took the *Moog* to the Speedway, the oil in the cooler mounted above the engine erupted like a geyser when they tried to start the car.

Left: Admiring Watson's new rear engine-design in Gasoline Alley. Only once during the whole month did it run and handle competitively. *IMS Photo*

Below left: When a gust of wind put Rodger into the wall during his warm-up laps before qualifying on Saturday of the last weekend, the crew had an all-night thrash to get the car ready to run on Sunday. Watson explained, "We fixed it, and never could get going again. Never could figure out why we couldn't get going. We finally took it to test, but it wasn't fast enough. Then, when we got to Milwaukee, we finally found out what was wrong with the car. The fuel pump had cracked, and it would run for a few laps and then it would slow down and it would leak fuel just enough to make it so wouldn't work. It didn't work good enough to run four laps of qualifying here at the Speedway. We missed the race." *IMS Photo*

Rodger Jr. visits with his father while they try to get the car up to speed on the afternoon of the last qualifying day for the 1965 Indy 500. He said, "Rodger felt like everything depended on him. He was angry that the car wasn't working, but he still refused to take other rides that were offered." *IMS Photo*

"We never had a good day with this race car. Absolutely none. I think we changed six or eight engines," he said.

While Watson was able to eventually solve most of the engine woes, the car's handling was diabolical. "Going down the back straightaway, my dad said he would take his left hand and hold it against the steering wheel and against his leg, and the car would dart left and right, changing lanes 15–20 feet going down the back straightaway without moving the steering wheel. The car would just dive and, as it would dive, it would change directions. It was just completely ill-handling," Rodger Jr. emphasizes.

While Foyt, Clark, and Gurney captured the front row with Foyt raising the track record to over 161 miles per hour, Rodger was frustrated on the first weekend of qualifying. He used two of his three allotted attempts, pulling in after one lap on the first one and explaining that he had bobbled in a turn, ruining his speed. Then Watson yellow-flagged his second attempt after laps at 154 and 155 miles per hour.

Don Branson qualified the team's second car, the *Wynn's Spl.*, at 155.5 on Sunday, after wrecking on Friday. Crew chief Jud Phillips got the car repaired and it curiously hadn't exhibited any of the handling problems shown by Rodger's mount.

Jud Larson, assigned Rodger's 1964 car now with an Offy installed, also made an unsuccessful attempt. There was even a fourth machine in the Wilke team's garage, a new roadster with a DOHC V-8 Ford bolted in front of the driver, who reportedly was Bobby Grim.

During the practice week before the second qualifying weekend, Rodger and A. J. made significant progress and Rodger's 157–mile-per-hour tour was top speed on Wednesday. His elation was increased when Diane presented him with their second child, daughter Robin, on Friday. Then it all came unraveled.

At 5:40 p.m., while taking his second warm-up lap before starting his qualifying run on Saturday, a gust of wind caught him and he brushed the wall exiting turn two. The *Moog St. Louis Spl.* then looped down into the inside wall, receiving severe front-end damage before sliding to a stop through the grass along the backstretch.

Watson had been through this before. While Rodger was checked and released from the trackside hospital, the car was quickly towed back to its garage, and by 7 p.m. the crew had stripped the damage and were preparing for a long night.

A dozen Leader Card crewmen removed the front end of Branson's qualified car and mated it with Ward's. While they

worked, Rodger paced the garage. He reportedly lost his temper with both the crew and kibitzers watching at the door. The job was completed by 3 a.m. on the last day of qualifying for the race. After a short night, the crew rolled the car out of the garage area for early practice. When Branson was asked if he was concerned about a critical part of his machine being borrowed, he replied, "If they don't give it back, I'm going to steal it."

After the first run, Rodger told A. J. that the car felt unsafe. It was quickly taken to the garage for chassis adjustments. Then he could only reach 150 miles per hour in the next practice and told Watson that the engine had a miss. The fuel filter was changed and, when that didn't solve the problem, Ford engineers joined the fight. After a 4 p.m. practice run, Rodger reported that the car was "worse than ever." The *Moog St. Louis Spl* was again rolled back to the garage where Watson went over it again, tightening and adjusting anything he thought might possibly be causing a problem.

With the late afternoon shadows from the main grandstand covering the front stretch, Watson sent Rodger out for a couple of practice laps to see if the crew had finally cured the problem. Before Rodger could get up to speed, though, Dempsey Wilson's car was pushed to the head of the qualifying

Above: At the wheel of the Mecum Racing Team Lola at Milwaukee in August. The George Bignotti-led team experienced a variety of mechanical problems that lasted through the end of the year. *Ken Coles*

Right: Rodger prepares for what would be his last Indy 500 in 1966. *IMS Photo*

line for an official attempt. Rodger returned to the pit lane, but instead of going to the Leader Card pit box, he stopped behind the last car in a qualifying line that had quickly formed. He knew that without testing the changes, the first laps at qualifying speeds could be risky. It would have to be an all-or-nothing effort, employing all of his experience, but there was no time left for anything else.

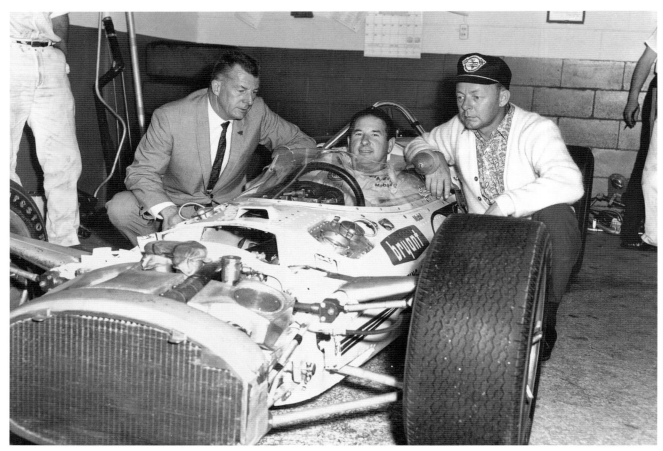

Right: Two Indy champions stop by the Mecom garage to check out Rodger's new Lola. Sam Hanks was USAC's Director of Racing and Jim Rathmann retired after the 1963 Indianapolis race. *IMS Photo*

Below: Rodger poses with the new Lola as Indianapolis opens. He scored his last championship victory at Trenton in April 1966 driving this Lola, which was powered by a supercharged Offy. *IMS Photo*

The line of cars moved forward with surprising quickness. Wilson spun and came in. Jud Larson only ran one lap in the car of another team. Mickey Thompson's new creation had its engine let go, and Carl Williams returned to the pits without starting his run. Just 45 minutes remained when Bill Cheesbourg turned four laps at 153.7 miles per hour and replaced rookie Mel Kenyon in the field. It was a last-ditch effort, but with qualifying ending at 6 p.m., teams were willing to accept any speed average that would put them ahead of the slowest car in the field.

Then Rodger rolled out for his last shot at making the race. The first two laps at 154.004 and 153.872 miles per hour, respectively, were faster than Cheesbourg's. But the car was slowing and the third lap was 153.244. The last lap was marginally better at 153.374, but still not fast enough to bump Cheesbourg. Bob Mathouser became the last car to take the green flag, but he slammed the wall and left debris across the track. As the gun signifying an end to qualifications was fired, the *Moog St. Louis Spl.* was being rolled back to the garage for the last time.

In hindsight, if the team had allowed Rodger to complete his second qualifying attempt, they would have made the starting field and had all of the next week to prepare the car to race, instead of worrying about qualifying. But that thought provided little comfort as the crew loaded their equipment.

Jimmy Clark won the 500 with a record speed of over 150 miles per hour. When Colin Chapman and the new Lotus visited victory lane, it was a triumph for the new paradigm of national championship racing. Parnelli narrowly edged Andretti for second.

The following Sunday at the Milwaukee 100 could have been a new day for the Wilke team, but it wasn't. Rodger was still frustrated by the car and could only manage an 18th fastest qualifying time. Then, exacerbating the situation, the oil filter blew while Rodger was lining up for the start and he was sidelined without completing a lap.

Next up was Langhorne. Since the dirt oval had been paved during the winter, Rodger decided to try the *Moog St. Louis* Watson again. But after Saturday's practice, he came into the pits and told Watson, "I don't like the car. I'm not going to drive today."

Watson found former motorcycle racing star Joe Leonard, whose All American Racers machine had flipped in a three-car tangle during practice, and put him in the car the next day. Leonard qualified ninth, but was caught up in the flaming accident that critically injured Mel Kenyon. Leonard helped

Indianapolis 1966; Formula 1 champions Graham Hill and Jimmy Clark might be asking Rodger for restaurant recommendations after a day of work. British racing writer Nigel Roebuck related the following story: "Jimmy started liking Indy more and more because he got familiar with it. Initially, he'd felt a bit lost there, I think, but he came to love it. I remember when we were at Indy in '64 that we all piled into his hire car one night, and went off to Sun Valley for the 'Little 500.' Unbelievable–a quarter-mile track with 33 starters, so the guy on the front row was in the exhaust pipe of the guy at the back! I remember in the race that Jimmy was up on his feet, cheering, he was so excited by it! He always wanted to drive a sprint car or a midget. By then he had got used to the States, to the way of thinking, the way of behaving, and became much more amenable to it. And he'd also realized, that financially, it was a very good deal!" *IMS Photo*

Mike San Felice and Charlie Musselman free Kenyon from the burning wreckage.

Looking back, Watson later allowed, "We were done for that day. That's how it happened, that's how he got away from us."

After Langhorne, it was announced that Rodger had left Leader Card Racing. Although Watson and the team continued

Chief mechanic George Bignotti focused his attention on cars of Hill and Jackie Stewart, both rookies, while preparing for qualifying and the race.
IMS Photo

to race for most of two more decades, their best days were behind them. At the same time, frustration at not lasting long enough to earn points in any of the races so far that season caused a row between Foyt and Bignotti, and the veteran mechanic departed the Sheraton-Thompson team.

When the tour reached Trenton, a Lola entered by John Mecom's new racing team was unloaded in the pits. Bignotti was heading the operation and he had Rodger for a driver. Unfortunately, their collective woes continued and a failed fuel pump kept them from qualifying for the race.

Mecom had big plans for his new team, most of which would become a reality over the winter. The new team got its first start when the road course at Indianapolis Raceway Park became the first road course competed on the championship trail in three decades. Rodger said the Lola was "strictly from Hungary" as he could only manage a 17th place qualifying time. But Bignotti found something to improve the handling before the start of the race, and Rodger hustled to ninth before the brakes began sticking in the turns, and his became the first car on the sidelines.

While Ward and Bignotti skipped the next event held on Atlanta's new high-banked speedway, Johnny Rutherford drove the Leader Card *Moog St. Louis Spl.* to his first championship victory. For Rodger, the nightmare season was beginning to approach its conclusion. Mecom Racing didn't own a dirt car, so by August he only had four events remaining on the championship trail. Their results didn't get much better and the record shows:

August 14, Milwaukee—overheated, finished 22
August 22, Milwaukee—mechanical failure, finished 23
September 26, Trenton—wreck, finished 23
November 21, Phoenix—fuel line, finished 15.

On December 6th, Rodger celebrated the end of his season by winning a USAC stock car race at Ascot while driving Bill Stroppe's Mercury.

1966

Over the winter, George Bignotti prepared the Mecom team for expansion at Indianapolis, with three new Lolas in house for Rodger, Scotland's Jackie Stewart, and sports car veteran Walt Hansgen. Rodger—the only one planned to run the full schedule and outfitted with a supercharged Offy instead of the Ford powerplant—started the season with an eighth place qualifying run at Phoenix. Running steadily, he was a solid fourth when Foyt and Andretti spun each other while battling for the lead, and Rodger found himself finishing second to Jim McElreath. Tragically, Hansgen later lost his life while testing a Ford Mk. II on the Le Mans course at the beginning of April.

Trenton was the last stop before Indy, and Rodger again timed the American Red Ball Lola-Offy eighth. Rodger was fifth by 40 laps, then passed Gordon Johncock and Jim McElreath to take third by the time Foyt pitted with a broken fuel line. On the 87th circuit, leader Mario Andretti had to stop for a tire

Rodger avoided the big pileup at the start of the race, but after 185 miles of nearly putting the Lola into the wall on every lap, he drove it to the garage, went home, and went to bed. *Photo courtesy of the Indianapolis Motor Speedway*

after running over debris, giving Rodger the lead. Then it began to rain, just shy of 100 of the scheduled 150 laps. When the rain increased the red flag stopped the race after 102 circuits, and Rodger had earned Mecom Racing its first victory.

Reigning F1 champion Graham Hill was lured back to the Speedway to fill the opening on the Mecom team left by Hansgen's death. This gave Bignotti two rookies to shepherd through practice and qualifying. They were assigned Lolas with DOHC V-8 Fords, while Rodger's Lola retained the more experimental supercharged Offy.

On pole day, Rodger was the first out to qualify, and he earned a spot in the fifth row with an average of 159.468. But things weren't going as smoothly as they seemed. There were problems with his car and he was getting very little attention from Bignotti, who seemed more interested in placing the spotlight on Hill and Stewart.

Rodger Jr. points out that his father had less practice time that month than ever. "Bignotti kept saying, 'Now Rodger, don't think that I'm not paying any attention to you. I know that you can sort this race car out, you don't need my full-time attention.' My dad didn't like that. In fact, he was a little resentful about it."

For the second time in three years, the race was stopped within minutes of showing the green flag. A couple of cars near the front of the field had been slow to accelerate as they crossed the starting line and the result was a pileup that involved 16 cars. The chaos had begun just ahead of the fifth row and Rodger and his Mecom teammates barely avoided being involved, as the whole sixth row was taken out. Among those eliminated before they reached the first turn were several favorites including Foyt, Gurney, and Branson.

When the race was restarted, Rodger tested his machine to see what he had for the day. With full tanks, it was as difficult as ever. Then the engine stalled when he made his first pit stop, on the 58th circuit. He held his breath until the 75th lap and then he turned down pit lane and drove the car directly to the garage area.

It turned out that there was a high spot in the Lola's steering rack. When Rodger set up for a corner, there was increasing resistance in the steering wheel as he tried to turn it to the left. When the car reached the apex of the turn, it would go past the high spot and, with the pressure Rodger was exerting, would quickly go further than it should have.

Opposite top: A champion's last ride. He was in his 16th year on the championship trail and, after finishing second and first in the season's opening events, it just wasn't fun anymore. *Ken Coles*

Opposite below left: Mario Andretti had two full seasons on the national circuit and was already on his way to his second championship. Some said that Andretti was hard on equipment, but he could win on any kind of course and in any kind of car. Foyt, Jones, and Andretti were the Ward, Bettenhausen, and Bryan of a new generation of racing fans. *Ken Coles*

Opposite below right: Bobby Unser had driven the supercharged V-8 Novi in his first three Indianapolis races and completed a total of just three laps in his first two Indy starts. But he would soon be winning regularly on the circuit and become a three-time champion at the Speedway. *Ken Coles*

Rodger Jr. says that the supercharged Offy made the situation much more dicey. "When he backed out of the throttle at the end of both long straightaways, it would load up with fuel really bad. So when he'd go to pick the throttle back up to go across the short straightaway, about that time it would go 'blub, blub, blub, blub,' then 'wwoooooowwwwwww!' just at the time he was at the high spot in the steering. He said that every lap, he almost put it on the fence for about the last 30 laps that he was out there. That was his last 30 laps in competition at the Speedway.

"The fact is he left before the race was over. He went down the pits into the garage, changed his clothes, got in his car, and went home. He went right to bed. Never said another word to anybody," Rodger Jr. explains. "He was very bitter. He was angry as hell about the whole thing."

A story in the June 9, 1966, issue of the USAC *News*, reveals, "'A long time ago, I promised myself that if racing ever ceased being fun, I'd quit. Well, yesterday it ceased to be fun. So, I'll be seeing you.' Thus, with a wave of his hand and tears streaming unashamedly down his cheeks, Rodger Ward rang down the curtain on an illustrious racing career that spanned 20 years." It noted that Rodger received a standing ovation from those in attendance at the victory banquet, including his fellow drivers and race winner Graham Hill.

Rodger enjoyed spending his time at the racetrack, whether he was talking business or just relaxing. Here he's with his good friends, Kenny Moran (center) and Marvin Farber (right). Moran was the head electrician at the Indianapolis Motor Speedway. Moran Electric was also an active sponsor of several cars. A long-time racing fan, Marvin Farber owned the Indianapolis area distributorship for Diet Rite and Nehi beverages. *Photo courtesy of the Kenny Moran Estate*

Epilogue & Postscript

A number of opportunities opened after Rodger retired, and he tried several of them. He was a particularly skilled people-person and, with his celebrity, he received many offers for a variety of "business deals." Some obviously didn't go as well as others, and at times he didn't make the wisest business choices. While he had success in a handful of situations, there wasn't any way to match the thrills and rewards of racing.

Rodger had been partners with A. J. Watson in an automotive and speed shop called Watson & Wards 500 Service, located just outside the main gate of the Speedway. In 1967, he opened a Firestone store a couple blocks away, on Crawfordsville Road. Rodger Ward Tire later expanded into several Firestone stores including one in Rosemead, California.

Rodger owned and operated Michigan's Owosso Speedway for several years. Here he enjoys being surrounded by racing fans. *Rodger Ward Jr.*

USAC called Rodger "automobile racing's number one ambassador," and as such, one of his many trips was to meet troops fighting in Vietnam. As he had with the Champion Spark Plug Highway Safety Team, he enjoyed bench racing with the troops, showing movies, and answering their questions.

When Ontario Motor Speedway opened in 1970, Rodger became Director of Public Relations. He was instrumental in developing Ontario's first racing programs, coordinating with the sanctioning groups, and initiating public appearances and promotions. Later, he was employed by the Industrial Films Division of Universal Studios. His job was to introduce Universal's ability to make documentary films to companies like Firestone.

His work for Circus Circus in Las Vegas gained some headlines. Initially hired to assist certain public relations programs, he went to work directly for Vice President Mel Larson. In time, Rodger ended up the manager of its boat racing program, running the unlimited hydroplane division.

But it was hard to stay away from his first love and, in the late 1970s and early 1980s, he owned and operated Owosso Speedway, a paved half-mile oval in Michigan. Rodger Jr. expresses the irony that many saw in that position: "Here's the legend of the Indianapolis 500—in my mind at least—and he's got a shovel in his hand and a rag in his pocket. He's changing light bulbs and cleaning toilets. That was my dad for you. He never saw himself doing it; it wasn't what he set out to do, but that's what it ended up being."

Later in life, Rodger worked with Composite Automotive Research, a Southern California firm that developed businesses manufacturing and selling a low-priced car in Third World countries.

After battling a debilitating disease, Rodger passed away in a hospice in Anaheim, California, on July 5, 2004 at the age of 83.

When Rodger wanted to become a pilot during World War II, his mother had written a letter to his high-school principal requesting a recommendation so Rodger would be considered for Officer Candidate School. The administrator replied with a short note, saying, "Anything I could say about Rodger wouldn't help him."

Rodger refused to give up. He found another route. He worked long hours while completing an aggressive college curriculum. In time, he became a fighter pilot. While this is an example of Rodger's knack for creating a negative impression, it also illustrates his determination to do whatever it took to achieve important goals he had set.

There are many stories about Rodger Ward. That's because there were many sides to his personality. Some said that he was a simple man. They were only seeing one side of him. In reality, Rodger was as complex as anyone and had a talent for presenting the side he thought would be the most successful in any situation.

When Rodger was racing, racing was his living. It was his paycheck. One of his downfalls was that as long as he had money, he spent it. An airplane, racing cars; at his peak, Rodger bought a lot of toys. He also liked to be on the cutting edge of fashion, and some thought he went over that edge. "My father had blue shoes," Rodger Jr. admits. "He had maroon, he bought a pair of bright green alligator loafers and burgundy alligator loafers, and he was at the Speedway one time after he retired wearing a bright green plaid sport coat and emerald-colored pants and his green alligator shoes. He was a sight to behold, my father. He spent [money] like there was no tomorrow."

"In those years, my father and mother were divorced when I was five," Rodger Jr. once recalled, "and he would come around every now and then, always with an armful of presents if he'd managed to get lucky. One thing different about my dad than most of the race drivers you know of, is my dad needed the money right up until the last Sunday—the last race. He needed the dough. Because he spent it all right as he went along."

There is no question Rodger had a weakness for partying, staying out late, having a good time, and enjoying the company of many women. While he was married five times, Rodger Jr. insists his father was simply a true romantic. Every time he had a new fiancée, it was going to last forever. "My dad fell in love. My dad fell in love with love," he explains.

Introduced by National Hot Rod Association (NHRA) founder Wally Parks to a young assistant in the association's headquarters, it was another case of love at first sight. In fact,

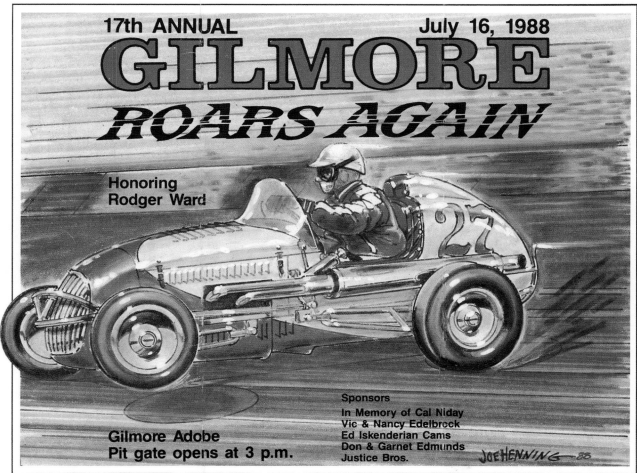

For many years, the annual Gilmore Roars Again party celebrated the Speedway that had been closed for more than half a century. This poster depicts Rodger's victory in the Edelbrock Ford for one of the affairs. *Don Radbruch Collection*

PRINTING COURTESY DON GONNELLA - EUREKA LITHOGRAPH

153

A reunion at Lime Rock in 1988 paid tribute to Ward's midget victory. Here, some of those who participated in the 1959 Lime Rock Formula Libre event and those who just came to celebrate pose with Rodger. In front, left to right: author Gordon White, Marty Himes, and Ward. In back, left to right: Pat Whitehouse, Roscoe "Pappy" Hough, and Boyd Hanauer. The Brenn midget that Rodger drove is the red No. 24 in the background, but in 1959, the car was light blue.
Photo courtesy of Gordon White

when Rodger made her Sherrie Ward in 1971, he had finally found the love that would last the rest of his life.

Rodger Jr. contends that his father's reputation as a drinker and wild man was overblown in most cases and grew as stories were told. "He said, 'I never really did drink that much. I was single, so I would be out. And I loved the women.' When he was at these joints, he would get a screwdriver at the beginning of the night and drink orange juice the rest. People thought he was a big drinker, but really he was just a playboy. Big drinkers stay big drinkers, and my dad wasn't much of a drinker. He wasn't good at drinking at all. He liked to stay out, goof around, and have a good time."

Above: Rodger was honored during a Western Racing Association (WRA) vintage program at Ascot in 1988. The Watson Leader Card National Championship dirt car was rolled out and Rodger was presented with a red helmet. Rodger listens as many of the old-timers are interviewed on the public address by Dan Fleisher, president of WRA at that time. Standing behind the right front tire in the black coat and white-and-black hat is midget racer, car owner and builder, and mechanic, Edgar Elder. Beside him is white-haired Ray Crawford, with Walt James standing next in the white pants and black coat. Dan Fleisher is interviewing the one-and-only Frank "Satan" Brewer. *Roy C. Morris*

Middle: Rodger listens intently as California Racing Association (CRA) official Evelyn Pratt gives him a bad time just before he is pushed off. *Roy C. Morris*

Bottom: Three legends: Rodger, the Leader Card dirt car, and the Ascot track. This was likely one of his last public appearances. *Roy C. Morris*

Family members found Rodger's 1959 Indy winner's trophy and the Levi Strauss trophy in a tin shed outside his brother's garage at an Ontario, California, welding shop. That was virtually all Rodger had left from his racing accomplishments. He wasn't a collector. While he was racing, he would give trophies to the trophy girl or a young fan, thinking there would always be another one the next weekend.

In 1992, Rodger was inducted into the International Motorsports Hall of Fame. The record book reflects a career that is brimming with accomplishment. He was a winner in one of the toughest, most competitive, and busiest midget eras ever. He won a national AAA stock car championship. Rodger started the Indianapolis 500 fifteen times and is among just fifteen drivers that have won the Memorial Day Classic more than once. In those fifteen years, he started 161 national championship events, won 27 events on the trail, and earned the point title twice. He finished 35.8 percent and won 16.8 percent of the races he started.

Those are just statistics, however, and they don't begin to capture the passion and skill that Rodger brought to the sport.

His teammate Len Sutton recalled, "Rodger was good at whatever he stepped into; he was going to run up front. Rodger had an awful lot of talent. There was no doubt in the world but that he knew how to get a race car around the track, he knew how to finish. Another driver that came along years later, by the name of Al Unser Sr. had a lot of the same kind of performance. The two of them got into a race car with the idea of moving up and doing it safely; of finishing races and winning your share.

"I hate to try to label anybody as being conservative in racing. Rodger knew the limits of his race car, the limits of the racetrack, and the limits of the conditions that they were running under. There again, that's why I compared him to Al Unser Sr., because Al Sr. had a phenomenal record of finishes, and finishing up front . . . a very heads-up driver. And that changed through the years. In the early years, Rodger wasn't noted for using his head. But in later years, I would say that he nailed it and always was a real good contender. In 1962, even though we weren't both starting in the front row or on the pole, when the newspapers came out to give the odds on who they thought would win the race, the newspapers awarded Rodger and me both 4:1 odds. I think Parnelli was 5:1 and Foyt was 7:1. Rodger, at that time, was considered a damn good contender anytime he bolted his helmet on."

Over four decades, A. J. Watson saw them all. He saw them win, lose, screw up, and sometimes die. He doesn't sugarcoat his words. Although Rodger and A. J. never became great social buddies, Watson is frank in speaking about his former driver. He says, "In the years he drove for me, he did real good. We made money and he put me on Broadway. I've probably lived on what I made from him for the rest of my life. He was a moneymaker; he finished all of the races at the Speedway when we were running there. And if you finish you can make money. We finished in the top four six years in a row and won it twice, so we did good there."

Rodger Jr. probably knew his father as well as anyone. Two things he has told me about Rodger stand out as I conclude this tale. Both seem so typical of the curly-haired fellow who loved a good time and could drive the heck out of a race car. Rodger Jr. reminds me that his father "never thought he was special, he always believed that he was the luckiest guy in the world."

Then he adds, "And he never quit believing in the pot of gold at the end of the rainbow."

Above left: Whenever Rodger went to a race, the Ward charm brought out the best in the fans. Here he's a guest at the Hoosier Hundred. He was also involved in a variety of business opportunities. One company he was involved with was based in San Diego. He explained, "It's been a year since I left there. I worked for a company that built factories and sold them to individuals in the Third World so that they could build a very inexpensive car that we designed. It was seven years ago that I took that job and moved down there. Then they wanted to move the company to the Philippines. I decided that it was not in my best interest to move to the Philippines." *Kim Turner*

Above right: Rodger Jr. relaxes with his father after attending the U.S. Grand Prix at Indianapolis in September of 2000. Rodger raced in the U.S. Grand Prix twice, at Sebring and Watkins Glen, in addition to the years that the Indy 500 was awarded international Grand Prix points. *Rodger Ward Jr.*

A. J. Watson joined Rodger when he was honored with a special day of ceremonies at the Speedway in May of 1999. Rodger frequently credited his persistence as being the critical element of his success. It was a quick and simple answer, but Rodger realized that for many years he raced in equipment that had little chance of winning and, consequently, how he often came close to giving up on his dream. *IMS Photo*

Popular Johnny Boyd's last Indy start was in the same race as Rodger's final run. In later years he became an unofficial ambassador in Gasoline Alley, frequently talking with fans, posing for photos, and hosting tours. *Ken Coles*

Bobby and Al Unser with Rodger in front of the Borg Warner Trophy in the Indianapolis Motor Speedway museum. The three Hall of Famers represent victories in nine Indy 500s and 94 national championship races. *Photo courtesy of the Indianapolis Motor Speedway*

Left: While helping with background information for this book, Rodger Ward Jr. relates, "The thing that's amazing to me is that I have the trophy from the Indy 500. And I have the Strauss Trophy. The Indy trophy from the 500 is a $20,000 trophy; that's what it costs to make it, but it's worth more than that now. Yet the thing that aficionados remember is the time he went over to Lime Rock and smoked everybody off. And that is a plaque! And even at that it's damaged. My dad didn't care about that stuff. 'Give the trophies to the trophy girl. I'll go get another one next week,' he'd say." *Rodger Ward Jr.*

Right: A memorial card from the celebration of Rodger's life at the San Diego Automotive Museum. *Roy C. Morris Collection*

Tribute To A Champion

Rodger Morris Ward
1921-2004

References

Angelopolous, Angelo. May 28, 1960. Race Driver's Wife. *Saturday Evening Post*.

Cadou, Jep. 1959. "Jep Cadou Jr. Calls 'Em," *Indianapolis Star*.

Clymer, Floyd. 1946–1969. *Floyd Clymer's Indianapolis 500 Mile Race Yearbook*. Los Angeles: F. Clymer.

Gates, Bob. 1995. *Hurtubise*. Marshall, IN: Witness Productions.

Gates, Bob. 2004. *Vukovich*. Marshall, IN: Witness Productions.

Indy Car Record Book, 1995 Edition. 1995. Championship Auto Racing Teams.

Kurth, Galen. "Getting Famous In Racing," *Flat Out* Magazine.

Montgomery, Bill. 1999. *Kurtis Kraft Midget: A Genealogy of Speed*. Marshall, IN: Witness Productions.

Popely, Rick. 1998. *Indianapolis 500 Chronicle*. Lincolnwood, IL: Publications International.

Saal, Thomas F. [not yet published]. *Damn Few Died in Bed*.

Scalzo, Joe. 2001. *The American Dirt Track Racer*. Osceola, WI: Motorbooks International.

Scalzo, Joe. 1999. *Indianapolis Roadsters 1952–1964*. Osceola, WI: Motorbooks International.

Sutton, Len. 2003. *My Road to Indy*. Portland, OR: Len Sutton.

Wallen, Dick. 2001 *Distant Thunder: When Midgets Were Mighty*. Escondido, CA: D. Wallen Publications.

Wallen, Dick. 1993. *Fabulous Fifties: American Championship Racing*. Escondido, CA: D. Wallen Publications.

Wallen, Dick. 2000 *Riverside Raceway: Palace of Speed*. Escondido, CA: D. Wallen Publications.

Wallen, Dick. 1997 *Roar from the Sixties: American Championship Racing*. Escondido, CA: D. Wallen Publications.

Wayne, Gary. 2001. *The Watson Years: When Roadsters Ruled the Speedway*. Marshall, IN: Witness Productions.

Yates, Brock. November 1999. "Bad Day at Lime Rock," *Car and Driver*.

Periodicals for General Information

Speed Age Magazine

Sports Illustrated

USAC *News*

USAC *Yearbooks*

Index